Embracing the Ties That Bind: Connecting with Spirit

Embracing the Ties That Bind: Connecting with Spirit

Carole J. Obley

To order additional copies of this book, contact:
Xlibris Corporation
1-888-795-4274
www.Xlibris.com
Orders@Xlibris.com
17546

Contents

PART THREE

Receiving and Reconnecting

*To my parents and grandparents who have
consistently demonstrated unconditional love;
to my spiritual guides, teachers, and angels
who have walked beside me in many lifetimes;
and to my clients who have mirrored to me time
and again the face of the Divine.*

Acknowledgments

The writing and publishing of this book has been made possible through the heartfelt efforts of the following individuals who have unselfishly given of their time and expertise:

Catherine M. Rosensteel, for the exquisitely done artwork, "The Dance of Life," on the cover of this book. You are blessed with an incredible talent, my friend.

A.J., whose invaluable computer technical knowledge and support enabled me to come out of the Stone Age and into the 21st century. Thanks for your unwavering personal support and encouragement during some of my darkest times.

Arlene Suvak, my friend and colleague, for early manuscript copy, proofreading and sound advice. You are truly an angel on earth!

Gina Mazza Hillier, for scrupulous professional editing. I always knew we'd work together upon our first meeting!

Rosy, for public relations efforts on my behalf, the "smile factor", and final manuscript editing. You've come a long way, baby and it shows.

Dan Compton, for being my friend and sounding board when the world (and the book) weren't going according to my plans. Thanks for not giving up on me.

Nancy Welsh, Sandra Tyler, and Vera Russell of Universal Life Healing Center, for being my human Way Showers on the metaphysical pathway. Without the Center, I would not be who I am today.

John Bruce Randall, for providing a place for me to do readings in the early days. Thanks for believing in me when I didn't believe in myself.

Frank of Mandala, for giving me the chance to be a part of your business and providing the opportunity for me to build rapport in the metaphysical community.

Finally, to the beloved souls who have graciously communicated with me from the world of spirit in countless sessions. You have brought much needed comfort and healing to your loved ones who have longed to hear from you.

Preface

I have always believed there is more to life than what I could detect through my five physical senses. From the time I was very young, I vigorously sought to delve beneath the surface of life and beyond the general knowledge I was taught in public schoolrooms and traditional religion. Long ago, I started asking questions that many of us ask in an attempt to gain spiritual understanding of our lives. *What is my purpose in life? What happens to my soul after I die? Have I lived before? Who or what is God?* Superficial answers to these and other questions have never satisfied my innate curiosity concerning the mysteries of the origin and journey of the soul.

More than fifteen years ago, I found myself magnetically drawn to the study of metaphysics through reading Edgar Cayce's writings on reincarnation, karma, and Atlantis. Since that time, I have sustained an incredible thirst for learning as much as I can regarding the nature of reality, the pre-existence of the soul, and what happens after we make transition into the afterlife. My pathway continues to expand from gathering knowledge for self-enlightenment to one of sharing the wisdom, communication and healing of spiritual guides, teachers and loved ones in spirit through readings, workshops, and hands-on healing. The blessings I have received from this work have been overwhelmingly joyful. Words cannot adequately capture the enormously rewarding feeling of love and gratitude I carry for being a channel for Spirit*. What a joy it is to deliver messages of love, forgiveness, and guidance from the spirit world. If given the opportunity I would not change a single facet of my life.

Some time ago, I began to receive messages from my spirit guides about sharing my experiences in mediumship, healing, and teaching intuitive development by writing a book. Interestingly, these messages coincided chronologically with some of the most spiritually challenging eras in our nation's history. On September 11, 2001, our collective consciousness shifted at an accelerated rate as a result of the terrorist attacks in New York and Washington D.C.; many of our individual and collective "shadow" emotions came to the surface to be examined and healed. Our sense of individual and national security, along with our trust, was incredibly challenged. What acts of anger and revenge were *we* capable of?

Recently, the Catholic Church has experienced major upheaval concerning moral, personal, and spiritual accountability for child sexual abuse, which has caused many people to re-examine their long-held feelings of sanctity and reverence towards the church and its leadership. The larger picture of these events leads one to believe that both political and religious systems that have been in place for centuries are now beginning to change in the process of evolving human consciousness. Although many people continue to look to organized religion and government for answers during this time of change, others have wondered where to turn for answers and reassurance in troubled times.

A sense of helplessness has sometimes surrounded people as they have asked, "What is the government going to do to fix the economic devastation from the terrorist attacks? Whom

* The word "Spirit", when capitalized, refers to divine consciousness, or what most people call "God".

can we trust to provide us with spiritual direction? What can be done to promote peace in the world today?" In the midst of this transition in our collective spiritual consciousness, there is uncertainty and unfamiliarity as we move into previously uncharted political and spiritual territory. This change is necessary and good. We are seeking to understand ourselves and the world from a new, more universal, yet personal perspective. We are hungry for answers to questions about what happens to us when we die, how our thoughts impact on the world, what relationships teach us about ourselves, and how we can naturally heal our bodies and emotions through non-invasive therapies. We are re-examining our relationship with money and coming to understand how we can experience prosperity without being self-serving. Most importantly, we are learning to turn *inward* to the divine truth of our souls for these answers. In this light, the question becomes "What can *I* do to heal myself, my relationships, my country, the world?"

From a metaphysical perspective, we're each responsible for our own soul. We create our reality moment by moment with our thoughts. The quality and vibration of those thoughts determine the state of our emotional well-being, physical health, the expression of our talents through a career, and many other characteristics of our daily lives. The realization that we, and we *alone*, are responsible for our lives is often threatening to our ego, which wants to blame someone or something for the inevitable disappointments and frustrations that life presents. Yet there comes a time in our spiritual evolution when personal accountability begins to become inescapably apparent. It is the point at which we stop pointing the finger at everyone and everything else and embark on the inner pathway that is necessary for us to come home to our souls and to our truth.

I have stumbled many times in the darkness of my own refusal to see the perfection of the light that emanates from my soul. At times, I have wanted to give up completely, not wanting to go into the unknown darkness any further. Yet I know that my truth includes the wisdom of knowing that the answers I seek lie within me because that is where God resides.

The ability to tune into and communicate with one's intuition and other dimensions of existence is something that each of us possesses. Until the age of 38, I was not aware of the extraordinary ability I have to communicate with other levels of consciousness beyond the physical. I share this story about the development of my mediumship abilities and how they have changed my life in the chapter, "My Story." Since the first time I consciously communicated with the spirit world, I have received and given confirmation of the continuity of the soul after death, what the spirit world is like, messages of unconditional love, and countless blessings of insight from the spirit people who have spoken in sessions with clients. When I lead intuitive development workshops, students are both amazed and pleased by the realization that they are able to perceive information without the use of their physical senses. There is a growing realization today that we must go beyond what can be proven by purely scientific means and the five physical senses. In this light, we are beginning to understand and develop our full potential as not only human beings, but as radiantly abundant *spiritual* beings. With the discovery of this potential comes the awareness of the connection we have with other worlds of spirit and the universe in general. Ironically, to find this connection, we turn not outward, but inward, to seek the wisdom of the Inner Voice, which is the voice of God residing within our soul.

We are spiraling to a level of evolution where we will ultimately embrace the full majesty of our divine gifts to create whatever we can envision. We will understand that it is our choice to live in either love (the essence of who we really are) or fear, (the voice of the ego that attempts to keep us "safe.") Each of us will come to appreciate and hold sacred our own soul, and in so doing, uplift and heal the rest of humanity. We will cherish and heal Mother Earth, who has unconditionally supported us in our evolutionary journey for thousands of years. World unity and peace will prevail as we band together as humans to improve the quality of life for all. This can only be accomplished through the remembrance and recognition of our innate divinity, which gives us the power to love and be loved. We will come to the realization that there is no separation between us and any other soul in the entire universe, especially loved ones who have passed into the world of spirit. Communication with other planes of existence will be accepted as a normal occurrence. I offer this book as a guide and inspiration to making this vision a reality on the planet and to assist you in the process of discovering your own truth. It is my sincere hope that your journey leads you into the most magical place of all—your own soul.

PART ONE

Giving and Releasing

1

MY STORY

Life is filled with irony and paradox, wouldn't you agree? Just when you think you have it all sorted out, something occurs to prove otherwise. One paradox that has always fascinated me concerns the concept of giving and receiving. What we give away freely, with an open heart, comes back to us many times multiplied, in many different forms. Because we all share a bond as humans, we receive insight, encouragement, and inspiration from listening to others share personal stories of life's experiences, challenges and triumphs. Relating our intimate stories of self-discovery inspires and encourages others in their search for self-understanding. For these reasons, I am sharing with you my story of the discovery of my mediumship abilities and my spiritual development with the hope that it will spark the realization within you that you are not alone on your pathway of self-discovery.

Synchronicities (experiences of divine timing), my spirit guides and a few miracles have brought me to a place of exhilarating expansion in my life where many closed doors have opened effortlessly. As I reflect on the pathway that has led me to unlock the mysteries of my own soul, I feel as if I have lived several lifetimes wrapped up in one. Before coming here this time, I suspect I contracted on a soul level to learn many lessons in the span of one lifetime.

A never-ending search to discover my life's purpose has been the source of constant change in my life. Because of the desire to explore what lies beyond this physical dimension, I have never really felt comfortable in any sort of societal or religious system that is restrictive in any way. From a very young age, I can remember incessantly asking the question "Why?" I was not, and never will be, content to stop seeking what lies just beneath the surface of life, the five physical senses, or the reasoning capability of the left-brain. I yearn to explore everything from the inside out, and often in direct opposition to the status quo.

Although I consider myself to be relatively stable and quite sensible, I have always been a person who has never done *anything* in life halfway. Testing and expanding the boundaries of life could be considered my full time occupation. Many times, this has worked in my favor, such as in the development of my psychic mediumship skills; other times it has worked to my detriment, as you will see.

Unlike some spiritual mediums, I was not aware of my psychic ability at a young age. I was born into an upper-middle-class family in the late 1950's. My father was an engineer and my mother, a secretary and homemaker. Despite growing up in a wonderfully stable and loving home, I felt like a loner much of the time. This took the form of feeling fundamentally different from others. Frequently, I felt like a silent observer of life and the world around me, often preferring the solitude of my bedroom to the company of others. For reasons unknown to me at the time, I felt isolated, confused and fearful of expressing my thoughts and emotions. Later I discovered that these painful emotions originated from the manner in which I viewed life from past life experiences

I had not healed. I was uneasy in social situations and therefore had only one close friend who was my next-door neighbor.

I remember the day I entered first grade, full of fear to leave the security of my home and the safe world of childhood fantasy I had known for six years. Despite my yearning to explore, I felt as if I was going away from all that was familiar to me. On that day, I clung to my mother's hand, reluctant to leave her side. The only consolation I had was the silent company of my favorite Barbie doll tucked away in my small red book bag. Little did I know later that day my teacher would take the doll from me and sternly announce, "We don't play with dolls in first grade!" When that happened I felt as if my last vestige of security had been stripped from me. Somehow I made it through that first day of school. I'm sure the knowledge that my mother was coming to pick me up at the end of the day instead of the school bus left me with some sort of security in knowing I would indeed return home.

One of my favorite things to do as a child was to stay with my grandparents on weekends. I loved all four of my grandparents and some of my fondest childhood memories are of spending time with them. I would often take long, leisurely walks with my father's mother. On one of these outings to a nearby bridge overlooking railroad tracks, Gram and I cut through a cemetery to reach the other side of the road. I was about ten years old. I remember walking through the cemetery, stopping to read the inscriptions on almost every tombstone as we passed. Some of the stones were quite old, dating back to the late 1800's. Others had photos of the deceased, which absolutely fascinated me. Letting go of my grandmother's hand, I walked closer to study the photos and dates of each person's birth and death. I recall curiously wondering about what this individual must have been like. Where did he grow up? What was his life like? How did he die? And where was he now? Did he know I was standing here looking at his grave? Some of the engravings indicated that the deceased was a child at the time of death. This made me sad to think that someone would die so young. It seemed very unfair. How could God allow such a thing to happen?

Even then, I longed to know what happens when we pass over. Do we go to heaven as I had been taught in Sunday school? Would we be reunited with our families after we passed? Do we play harps and sit on clouds with the angels like the TV shows I had seen? Curious as I was about death and the afterlife, I harbored a fear surrounding the entire subject. I dreaded going to funeral homes when a family member died, often having nightmares after viewing the body. Alone in my room, I would sometimes sleep with the small bedside lamp on, too afraid to imagine what I might see if the room was completely dark.

Death wasn't the only thing I feared as a child. I was also anxious and uncertain about school most of the time. Even though I excelled academically throughout most of my school years, I seemed to always be filled with fear. Of what I was not sure, although social situations seemed to accentuate it. Because I had few friends, I spent most of my time in my room listening to music on my little Westinghouse 45 record player, reading, and playing with my dolls. On Sundays, I attended a Protestant church with my family, going to Sunday school and sometimes the regular services. Despite having to get up early to attend, I really enjoyed Sunday school.

Miss Johnson, my teacher, required us to memorize the books of the Bible in order, both Old and New Testament. I remember reciting them at home, knowing that we would be quizzed on them the following Sunday. We were also required to learn the 23rd psalm and the Lord's Prayer because we recited them each week before class began. I loved the 23rd psalm because it gave me a sense of security and peacefulness. Miss Johnson was a schoolteacher during the week and ran her Sunday classes much like a regular schoolroom. We sat in rows and were strongly discouraged from engaging in chatter during class. She prepared us for confirmation, a serious commitment to church membership that entailed the adult responsibility of understanding and serving God primarily from the knowledge given in the Bible and taught in the church.

During the years spent with Miss Johnson, I learned many things about the Bible, religious teachings, and the life of Jesus. I made new friends and attended the church social events that were offered. Yet I remember feeling lost, spiritually unfulfilled, and unable to really *feel* God. I thought I must have been missing something, especially since I tried so hard to connect with Him through the Bible and the church. It was as if I left Him behind in the Sunday school classroom each week when I physically left the church building. At the same time, I was aware of feeling different and isolated from my school peers, no matter how hard I tried to fit in. I seemed to look at the world differently than they, even in the simplest of matters. Every question I asked about the lessons I was taught in Sunday school and the public school classroom prompted ten more questions in my mind.

I had an unquenchable thirst to investigate the paranormal—particularly ghosts and after-death phenomenon. UFOs intrigued me to the point that I read any book or watched any movie I could find on the subject. No one else I knew seemed to share my fascination with the unexplained, which intensified my feelings of uniqueness and loneliness. I just couldn't relate to most people around me, despite my efforts. Music and books provided the much-needed solace I lacked from my social interactions. The singers of the top forty songs on the radio and the characters in my books seemed to know and understand my feelings of isolation. The bare bleakness of everyday life bored me compared to the fascination I found in exploring other realms of existence. I fantasized about beautiful fairies visiting my back yard, leaving gifts of glittering gold jewelry and the most exquisite toys for me to play with. I craved the magical and the unusual in everything. I became determined to find it.

Feelings of Loneliness

By my teen years, the feelings of loneliness and separation became so unbearable that I began to seek escape in recreational drug use. A boyfriend in high school introduced me to marijuana. It and I became best friends. Under the influence of the drug, I could reach and tune into the expanded states of consciousness that I had merely read about in books. I believed smoking it gave me the insights I so craved, especially about what lies beyond the physical realm. It also enabled me to feel "cool" and part of the "in" crowd, which I desperately longed to be. By this time, my taste in music had changed to include more rebellious musical groups that reflected my inner "angst." I became a "partier", seeking relief from feelings of alienation and low self-esteem in substances, people, and things, which offered me a temporary remedy from my everyday malaise. Still, I never felt so alone. Despite my drug use, I managed to get inducted into my high school's honor society and became co-editor of the school newspaper. The latter I did with some reserve because of my inclination to want to go beyond the basic facts that most journalism presents. Editorials were my favorite pieces to write because they allowed me to articulate a more personal perspective and to inject a little creativity into the process. They also gave me the opportunity to present new ideas and a fresh outlook on timely topics of interest to the student body. If I had been more introspective, I would have realized that writing offered me a productive outlet for my intrigue with extraordinary reality. Instead, I chose to continue on the pathway of comfortable confusion that I had become accustomed to.

Upon entering college, I made the decision to major in English. I had always loved to read and it seemed like a natural subject for me to pursue. I decided to take education classes so I could teach it. I changed my mind after having a discouraging experience student teaching at a local secondary school. The curriculum didn't incorporate enough room for creativity or personal expression. I felt hemmed in by others' expectations. Nonetheless, I decided to continue in English as my major.

Despite maintaining excellent grades, I had immense trouble in my personal life. It was not easy to make friends on campus, and it really didn't interest me much to join school organizations. I spent time in the record stores and pubs that served the student population. Just prior to high school graduation, I had discovered the warm, anesthetizing effects of alcohol and the long-sought feelings of self-worth and confidence it seemed to give me. In college, I attended many campus parties where I would seek refuge in the familiar comfort of drinking and in the company of the most "on the fringe" and extreme people I could find. *They would understand me*, I thought. All I wanted was someone with whom to share my thoughts and feelings. That "someone" never appeared because I wasn't emotionally open enough to welcome anyone into my life. I began to blame others for my despair because I was unwilling to take an honest look at myself. I projected the burden of my feelings onto others in my life and the world in general. I wondered why life was so difficult and empty. I was filled with self-pity.

Regardless of my personal turmoil, I graduated with honors. Although I had a degree in English, I had absolutely no idea what I was going to do with my life. This was mainly due to the fact that I remained unaware of the purpose of my life. Over and over, I asked myself the same questions: *Why am I here? What do I have to offer the world? Where do I belong in the world?* I felt as if I was sleepwalking through life. It seemed as if everyone else had life figured out but me.

Age of Reckoning

After graduation, I continued to seek comfort in alcohol. At the age of 22, it was my constant companion, and I allowed my feelings of isolation to control my outlook on life. *No one understands me*, I would moan to anyone who would listen. I had few friends as I continued to wallow in feelings of self-pity and anger. Exactly who I was angry with I was not sure, but certainly it was *somebody's* fault that I felt alienated. My life felt meaningless and out of control. I had no conscious recognition of a spiritual awareness or identity. Instead, I sought to stretch every boundary I had grown up with, been taught about, or previously respected. I lost a lot of sleep, most of my self-respect, and all common sense. I had hit bottom.

By the age of 25, I realized I couldn't continue living the way I had and sought private therapy and 12-step programs for my drinking. With the help of therapists and many others in recovery, I was able to stop drinking. Three to four times a week, I attended meetings where I heard others tell their personal recovery stories. Some of the stories were quite fascinating and I made many new supportive friends. But the most intriguing part for me was at the beginning of each meeting when the 12 steps were read. They seemed to call out to me and invite me to embark on the wondrous journey of understanding myself for the first time. I began to diligently "work" the steps and speak at meetings about my life and the feelings that I tried to escape through drinking. As I look back on this period of my life, I realize with a definite sense of gratitude that I chose to discover myself and my spiritual identity through the lessons of addiction and recovery. If it were not for the unconditional love and support of the 12-step groups, I probably would not be serving Spirit through my work today.

I was well on the road to recovery when I landed my first job in years, a presser at a dry-cleaning plant. As part of my continuing recovery, I read and studied books about women's issues, self-empowerment and healing. I knew that I had to change from the inside out because what I was doing before in my life simply wasn't working. Period. Even though I had expressed my feelings and experiences at 12-step groups, I still desired to reach and explore deeper levels of my core identity, such as my awakening spiritual awareness, with others who would recognize and validate my perceptions. I needed to believe I had a purpose in life and was lovable, yet I didn't actually believe these things myself. I can remember thinking that I want to be *someone*. I longed to fit in and be like everyone else in my life, yet I held a deep feeling that people would not accept me as I was. Or so I believed.

My Own Business

Over the course of ten years, I gradually developed greater self-esteem and a sense of personal power from attendance at recovery meetings, self-help books, and introspection. I read and studied metaphysical books to satisfy my hunger to learn about alternate concepts of reality. I noticed that my feelings of separation and isolation lessened in direct proportion to the amount of time I spent listening to and sharing with others of like-mind in recovery. I realized I was *not* alone and never had been. What I had felt and thought for many years was an illusion that I had allowed to nearly destroy me. My self-identity slowly evolved from being the loner who was emotionally unfulfilled to one who was connected to others and in control of life. This, I thought, was a *miracle*.

In my mid-thirties, I was offered the chance to own and operate a local laundromat and dry cleaning establishment, which had not done well under the previous owners in recent years. I had accumulated experience in the business of fabric care from working in several different positions in the dry cleaning plant. I jumped at the offer, mostly because I saw it as an opportunity to take charge of my own destiny. I was up for the challenge. Regardless of my emotional turmoil, I have always been true to the characteristics of my astrological sun sign of Capricorn, fiercely determined to succeed and entirely perfectionistic. My own business would be the perfect outlet for my need to feel successful, in control, and financially secure. My business partner, Kathy, and I signed the lease for the building and began the job of cleaning the place.

Things went reasonably well for a year or so as Kathy and I rebuilt the business. The prior owners had allowed the place to sink into disarray and had employed less than reputable business practices. This was the reputation we had to overcome, which was no small feat. In addition to having the daily maintenance of the equipment and machinery we used for operation, we had all of the regular duties of attending to customers, pressing clothes, and running commercial laundry accounts. Most days I put in 12 hours, falling into bed exhausted each night. My social life was non-existent. A vacation was out of the question because of the constant attention required by the business. I had no real identity outside of the business and I felt spiritually disconnected. I *became* the business. I started to question whether this was what life was about—working, eating, and sleeping. As I calculated each day's monetary intake of the business, I silently set my expectations on the next day, hoping things would get better. They didn't. In fact, they got worse.

Kathy and I struggled to keep our heads above water with the many financial demands of building a business. The utility bills alone were staggering, as were the costs of rent and repairing the equipment. It was all we could do to make a small profit by the end of each month, despite both of us spending numerous hours working every day. We tried many avenues to manage financially, including cutting costs and taking on larger commercial accounts. It was still not enough to pull the business out of debt. At the age of 35, I once again grappled with feeling that life was essentially meaningless. I was merely existing, not living. I was working my life away, with very little to show for it. And then everything changed overnight with a phone call.

A Phone Call That Changed My Life

At about three years into running the business, I had grown accustomed to the routine of working 12-hour days. Sometimes I worked even longer, depending upon how quickly we finished the commercial accounts. We were still struggling financially and seriously considered taking out a business loan to repay some of the debt we had accumulated from the high utility bills. I was frustrated and disillusioned. I have always been a person with large reserves of determination. At this point, however, I found my fortitude running precariously low.

One night in March of 1995 I came home from work, relaxed, and went to bed as usual. Around 4:00 a.m. I awoke to the sound of the telephone. A feeling of alarm went through me as I sleepily trotted into the other room to answer it. On the other end was Rick, my business landlord. "Carole, you'd better come quickly—the building is on fire! The fire department is already down there. I'll see you there," he said. Shock waves pulsed through my mind and body as I threw on the nearest clothes and shoes I could find. I ran to my car and drove to the building, which was only two miles away.

I prayed that the damage would not be extensive. I must have thought of a dozen things at the same time that morning; it is amazing how many thoughts can bombard our consciousness in a few minutes in an emergency. I thought about the start-up money I borrowed from my brother and how I hadn't yet paid it back. I thought about the fish aquarium in the building and whether the fish would survive the fire. I silently calculated the amount of customers' clothing we had in the store. Most of all, I let my mind go back to the prior evening and particularly the condition of the building when I left it. What had gone wrong? Did I forget to turn off something? Had a customer left a cigarette burning that had ignited the place? Why hadn't I checked everything more closely? I felt guilty without even knowing the cause of the fire. Then I thought *it's probably just a little fire tnat started a short time ago and will be quickly put out.* My heart sank as I rounded the bend and saw the scene, which included about three fire trucks and two emergency vehicles, all actively engaged in extinguishing the fire.

It took about an hour to completely put out the flames. As I walked through the debris, it was hard to tell that it was the same neat, tidy place that I had spent many hours in each day. All but the equipment was a pile of rubble. The TV set was a melted ball of plastic. Most of the customer's clothing and the commercial accounts were extensively smoke and water damaged. There was no way we could remain open for business. It would take months to rebuild. I was devastated. In an attempt to retain our customers and the commercial accounts, we worked out of a nearby plant that graciously allowed us to temporarily use their facilities. Slowly we picked up the pieces. I felt angry, confused, and totally defeated. Little did I realize at the time that I stood at a major crossroads in my life, one that led to the pathway of my life's true purpose.

Phoenix Rising From the Ashes

After the fire, it became apparent that Kathy and I had to decide whether to rebuild the business or move on. To complicate matters, there was a dispute concerning the cause of and the liability for the fire. We were able to settle the customers' claims for their damaged goods, but received little compensation for our lost wages. Additionally, I had been unable to repay my original start-up costs. It just did not seem feasible to rebuild. All things considered, we decided that it was time to move on.

For several months I wallowed in self-pity, feeling depressed and useless. I hadn't a clue as to which way to turn in my life or what type of employment to seek. Once again, life seemed meaningless and dull. Because I had worked so many hours in the business with practically no social life, I found myself without the support of friends in my time of crisis. I began to say vague prayers for guidance, not really expecting any answers, yet asking nonetheless. I went on a few job interviews. Still nothing happened. For six months, I wrestled with which direction my life should take. At one point I remember thinking angrily that I wish someone would assign me a job, any job, so I could cease struggling with the question of what to do with my life. I resigned myself to working on the commercial accounts from the now defunct business. I was unhappy, nearly broke, and—to borrow a phrase from 12-step programs—spiritually bankrupt.

One day, a friend * I had not seen in quite some time called to see how I was doing. After pouring out my heart to her, she casually told me about a metaphysical healing center she'd recently visited in a nearby town. I asked her the name of it. "It's called the Universal Life Healing Center," she replied. I listened with some interest as she described the center's Sunday services, healing sanctuary, and supportive fellowship. Then she invited me to come along the following Sunday. I took down the directions, all the while not really planning on attending. By next Sunday, however, I changed

*Several years ago this dear friend passed on in a car crash. From my heart, I send her the deepest gratitude and blessings for passing this information onto me since Universal Life Healing Center has been a catalyst in my spiritual development.

my mind and decided to give the center a try. What did I have to lose? Things could not possibly be worse in my life.

Started several years earlier by three female ministers, Universal Life was housed in a former Baptist church building. According to the statement of beliefs contained in the hymnal, it was founded to promote the concepts of universal brotherhood and healing. Classes on metaphysical topics, book study groups and private sessions for healing and spiritual readings were offered on a regular basis. There were about 25 members who attended weekly. Most of what I experienced while there was vaguely familiar to me. Although I had always been interested in spiritual metaphysics, I had never taken the opportunity to take classes in it. The Sunday service consisted of a guided meditation, a presentation on the metaphysical meaning of healing, several songs with a universal spiritual theme, then a gentle laying-on of hands. Although I found the rest of the service appealing, I felt incredibly drawn to the healing part of the service. We were encouraged to go to the healer of our choice. I chose a minister who happened to be standing nearest to me.

During the five-minute healing, I felt indescribable warmth, tingling and most of all, love. After the healing, the minister said quietly, "In your heart chakra, I sense a beautiful red rose just about to bloom. It represents all the love you have inside to offer the world." Upon receiving this message, I felt more strongly connected to God than ever before. I began to sense a purpose for my life and a desire to find out what it was. When I sat down, I felt like a different person who was somehow fuller, happier, and loved unconditionally. I decided to stay for fellowship after the service.

The Acceleration of My Pathway

Soon after going to that first service, I began to attend the center regularly. One Sunday, I decided to nose around the center's library, which contained many books on metaphysical topics such as healing, reincarnation and karma, the chakras, and life after death. Each week, I checked out a few books and borrowed guided meditation tapes so that I could learn how to reach more expanded states of consciousness for healing. Perfectionist that I am, I felt that I was not "doing" meditation correctly. I even asked one of the ministers about what I was "supposed" to feel and see during meditation. She put her arm around my shoulders and quietly said with a smile, "Carole, it's not possible to fail meditation." Obviously I was unaware just how conditioned my left-brain thinking had become. Since those early days, it has become an inside joke at the center that if "Carole could open her right brain enough to become a healer and medium, anybody can!" I have come to appreciate the value of my rational side much more than before. In many ways, this logical side of me enables me to be a more effective teacher for people who take my psychic-intuitive development seminars. The best teachers serve by power of example.

During the first several years I attended the center, I was absolutely determined to learn everything I could about mediumship, the journey of the soul through eternity, and metaphysical healing. I longed to do something more meaningful than my current job, but still wasn't sure what that might be. In an effort to find out, I took many classes that were offered at the center. I felt an increasing desire to facilitate the spiritual healing that took place in the center's healing sanctuary, the same type of healing I'd experienced during my first visit there. I had already taken the necessary training to become attuned to Reiki, a Japanese healing modality in which the healer channels universal life-force energy. I performed Reiki every chance I got, especially distance treatments, which involve the use of special symbols to focus the healing energy. But I didn't want to stop there. I wanted to be one of the healers who stood up front every

Sunday, serving Spirit by being a healing channel. So, in the typically intense way that I approach life, I set my sights on training to begin my apprenticeship as a spiritual healer.

Magically, every time I set my intent on taking a class to intensify my training, the funds to do so suddenly appeared. Sometimes, it was amazing how quickly this happened. For example, when I made the decision to study Reiki, the money for the class was gifted to me within two days by my grandfather. When I later took intensive mediumship training at Delphi University in Atlanta, I was able to pay for the entire tuition from funds that were given to me from a friend. Many people who have come to me for readings have shared similar stories of how their finances miraculously supported their spiritual pathways. I firmly believe that when we meet with our divine purpose, the very sky will open up to help us move more quickly along the intended pathway for our soul's growth. This is what I call "divine acceleration," a phenomenon that we all can experience when we remove our personal resistances of doubt and fear and begin the healing process.

Two years after my initial visit to Universal Life, I was doing spiritual healing there on a regular basis in the healing sanctuary. I had completed all of the preliminary training and was now an apprentice to a more experienced healer. I loved doing the healings, which consisted of a 20-minute laying–on of hands for people who came to the sanctuary. During this time my reluctance to do anything halfway reared its head again and I began to feel as if I was inept as a healer. Since spiritual healing is mostly an intuitive process, the healer often relies on spirit healers to give psychic impressions of the client's energy field. I felt I was not receiving detailed enough psychic impressions of an individual's energy field. On top of that, my healing spirit guides were *not* being clear enough with me about the placement of my hands. I felt as if I was not receiving these impressions at all. In frustration, I asked them why they were not giving me enough information. Their reply came through one of the other healers who told me to be patient and let the process develop naturally. My left-brain was once again working overtime, hoping to be paid extra! I persisted in doubting my intuitive ability. Finally one of the ministers told me in a curt tone to stop asking so many questions and simply *trust* the process. I tried to defend myself, although I was genuinely concerned that I would never be able to do this work that required me to give up so much control of my own thinking. I was wrong.

Delphi

Soon after beginning work in the healing sanctuary, I decided to further my spiritual training by attending intensive mediumship classes at Delphi University near Atlanta. All of the ministers at Universal Life had attended and gave it favorable reviews. The classes for the first level in mediumship training lasted one week. I immediately made the decision to go because I had such a strong desire to develop and expand my abilities. My discovery of Delphi is a perfect example of synchronicity. Had I not been attending Universal Life, I probably wouldn't have known about Delphi. I believe we are miraculously ushered to the people, places, and situations that help us to transform our lives according to our individual divine blueprint. When we act in complete faith that everything in our lives happens according to this plan, we orchestrate our lives with much less resistance than if we try to run the whole show with our egos as the conductors.

I left for Delphi six weeks after hearing about it. I had an uneasy but welcome feeling that my entire life was about to change. I shared a room in the campus housing with my friend Wendy whom I had met in Lilydale, New York, a spiritualist community where we had both taken classes. It was reassuring to know someone in a strange place. I hadn't been away from home for an extended period of time since college, and I could feel my anxiety begin to rise the minute the plane departed from Pittsburgh. In an undefined way, I felt as if I was leaving behind everything that was familiar to me. As the coming week would prove, indeed I was. I had no idea how transforming my experience at Delphi would be, although one thing was certain: I went with a compelling desire to stretch my personal boundaries to communicate more clearly and deeply with Spirit. My spiritual memory banks were about to be activated in a profound way. I knew this was something I *must* do.

The week consisted of intensive training in the recognition and development of mediumship skills. We began each morning with a group meditation, followed by breakfast. We then had morning and afternoon classes with lunch in between. After dinner, we finished the day with a three-hour evening class. Experiential in nature, the classes were designed to build trust in receiving and interpreting the inner voice of Spirit. We worked in small group settings, which allowed for individual attention. Many of the exercises were designed to break down self-imposed barriers that prevent us from connecting with the inner voice of the Divine. Tears of joy and relief welled up each time I felt an emotional breakthrough. At times, I became defensive and wanted to quit when a classmate inadvertently "pushed my buttons." *I can do this*, I thought. *It's only a week.*

At mid-week, we were given half a day off to explore the beautiful mountain setting around the school. I gathered natural crystals from the wooded areas on the ground as souvenirs to share back home. As I walked, I thought about where my life was headed and why I felt so compelled to study spiritual mediumship and healing. *Have I done this before in a past-life? Is that why I'm so drawn to it?* I wondered why I felt inexplicably guided to follow this pathway beyond "normal" reasoning and break through the boundaries of fear that had kept me in place for so many years. I resolved to find the answers that would unlock the mystery of this calling.

That week, I became keenly aware of the presence of my spiritual guides and teachers. They gently introduced themselves to me in stages so I would not be startled by them. Earlier in the week our class meditated to connect with "One Who Cares"—a guide who came in unconditional love. During the experience, I sensed a beautiful, loving woman who handed me a large red heart. I was overwhelmed with peace and joy as she gently reached out her hand to welcome me "home." She communicated to me that I needed to trust more and remove the shield in front of my heart to allow love to flow. Although I still don't know her name, I recognize her loving presence with me even now. Later in the week, we took what are called "trips", one-on-one sessions with an instructor that are designed to build trust in the process of intuitive development. This is where I met Ra, my magnificent lion guide. During the session, he revealed himself to me in my mind's eye by standing directly in front of me. At first I thought I was imagining him, because it seemed so improbable that I had a lion as a spiritual guide. My instructor encouraged me to trust what I saw. Since that first meeting, I have seen Ra many times—especially when I am in need of courage during challenging times. Other guides have introduced themselves to me over the last several years. One of these has been Rolf, my joy guide, whom I describe later in the chapter on "Spirit Consciousness." During dark periods of doubt and fear, I have found his presence to be comforting and reassuring.

On the last day of class, each student was expected to give two mini-readings for volunteers who come to the school from neighboring areas. I was afraid of not being able to do the readings, but realized that I was once again allowing fear to control my thinking. It was a pattern that I desperately wished to release. By the time I was finally alone in a small reading room with two complete strangers, I was determined to prove to myself that I could apply all I'd learned that week, especially the need to trust in the validity of the information I received from Spirit. I decided to walk directly through the fear and summoned my spirit guides to help me. I greeted my first "client" nervously but cheerfully and began the reading.

To this day, I have no fixed ideas about how mediumship actually works. From the time I did that first formal reading, I have been astounded by the amount of accurate information, guidance and healing that Spirit is able to impart through the channel of a medium. The first client I read, an older woman with a friendly demeanor and a broad smile, confirmed almost everything I said. It was the most magnificent, magical feeling I have ever experienced in my life. Spirit gave me many specific details that I couldn't have logically known about this woman. The most baffling aspect of the whole thing was the experience of starting a sentence, only to have Spirit finish it without any forethought on my part. This has happened to me many times since in readings, and it never ceases to amaze me. I begin to speak, not knowing exactly what I'm going to say; what comes out is invariably accurate and applies to the topic or person at hand. This is what is possible when we are able to release the judgment of our left or rational brain. Spirit is then able to speak to us through our intuition, which is a function of our right or feeling brain.

Many people ask me how psychic information comes to me when I do readings. The best way I know how to describe the reception of this information is by using an analogy. Suppose that you are standing in front of a painting covered with a dark cloth that you have never viewed before. Imagine that someone removes the cloth, as you continue to stand in front of the painting. What is your "gut" response to the painting? What feelings does it evoke in you? What is your overall impression of it? Does it elicit memories of your life?

The sensations and thoughts that I receive in a reading come through in much the same way as the experience of viewing the painting for the first time. The impressions I receive are interpretations of clients' energetic "canvas" as they are revealed to me through attunement to their soul.

The last night at Delphi was pure elation and joy. I felt a great sense of accomplishment and a renewed sense of connection with my purpose. Most of all, I felt fully *alive* as if I belonged with the family of humanity, possibly for the first time in my life. I packed my bags, said goodbye to Wendy, and flew home. It was a new day.

Getting Out There

Upon my return from Delphi, I posted a sign-up sheet for readings at Universal Life. More than ten people immediately signed up. At graduation, the instructors told us we needed to give five readings at home in order to receive our certificate of mediumship. I ended up doing 15 readings. I sent in the forms and received an official gold seal for my graduation certificate from Delphi.

As I continued to do readings, I began to feel an incredible sense of unconditional love and upliftment. I felt more aware, alive, strong, and connected to life. There was definitely more going on here than met the eye; I still had no idea where I was going with all of this newfound awareness. I loved being in the space between the physical and spirit worlds, acting as a translator and mirror for clients and their guides and loved ones in spirit. I began to get a good reputation for being accurate. People started to come to me by personal reference. The depth and scope of the readings continued to expand. Up until this time, I had not charged money for my readings because I felt they were still part of my apprenticeship. However, I soon discovered that people attach little value to free services. I felt emotionally drained and questioned whether I needed to seek a steady job that offered the certainty of a regular paycheck. I asked my guides for help.

Soon after, I was offered an opportunity to read professionally at a metaphysical bookstore in Pittsburgh. Although I jumped at the chance, I still had doubts about my abilities. What if I was wrong about some of the information I gave people? What if I unintentionally hurt someone by giving incorrect guidance? Perhaps I had just been lucky up until now and the people I had read for were just being kind in verifying the information I had imparted. Again fear began to get to me.

Today, as I look back on these and other feelings of doubt I had, I am grateful to have experienced them. They have enabled me to get in touch with the lack of trust many people feel when they begin to open their intuitive senses. I completely understand the sense of disbelief many of my students of intuitive development experience when they begin to receive their initial intuitive impressions during the developmental exercises we do in class. As one who has walked the path, I try to allay their misgivings with reassurance and loving support that is so necessary to validate the inner voice of intuition. I have found that without trust, it is nearly impossible to learn intuitive development. When I was starting out, I put undue emphasis on attempting to prove the accuracy of my readings. I now know that any information that I receive, no matter how insignificant it seems to me, is meaningful in some way to clients. Even though they may not be able to validate it at the time, I often receive confirmation of the information's accuracy from them later. If it's one thing I've learned doing my work, it's trust.

I began to read at the bookstore one day a week and kept two other part-time jobs to pay the bills. I wasn't able to trust *that* much! But before long I had weekly appointments at the store—sometimes as many as four readings in one afternoon. Despite my doubts about attracting clientele, Spirit was certainly providing. Each reading I did provided me with a renewed sense of confidence in my abilities and enabled me to open to a deeper level of trust. When I received feedback from clients on the positive effects of the experience, I felt incredible satisfaction that I helped someone grow spiritually. I sincerely wanted to make mediumship my full time profession.

I returned to Delphi to take further training in mediumship and spiritual healing. After completion of all of these classes, I became ordained as a metaphysical minister, a step that was beneficial in starting my own practice of counseling and healing. The second trip to Delphi was not as pleasurable as the first; I was sick the entire time with the flu and was barely able to attend all of the classes on past life regression, hypnosis, and healing modalities. Determined to make it through the curriculum, I forced myself to go to all but one of the classes. I recognized that being ill was due to two interrelated causes: fear of going to a deeper level of commitment with my work and to getting in touch with a past life experience in an Egyptian prison that had adversely influenced me for lifetimes. I had been a prophet who was unjustly persecuted for empowering others with spiritual information. I realized that this unhealed experience was the root cause of the feelings of isolation and sadness I had felt most of my life.

My second visit to Delphi also enabled me to learn a valuable healing tool to use in my practice—past life regression. Years earlier, when I read Edgar Cayce's past-life readings, I was intrigued by how present day illnesses and emotional problems often have their origins in unhealed past-life traumas. I have found the tool of regression to be invaluable in helping clients release deeply held patterns of fear that cannot be healed through other techniques.

About 18 months after becoming certified, I was offered an opportunity to give readings on a local radio station. It was near Halloween when all mediums become more in demand. The show aired very early in the morning and I had to drive to the station at 4:00a.m. The night before, I was extremely nervous about what questions I would be asked by the DJs and what would happen during the readings. I had done phone sessions for clients and found that the voice vibration of the individual on the other end transmitted a wealth of information about the individual. I could read just as clearly over the phone as in person; it seemed to make no difference. Yet I was concerned about doing this on the radio, with thousands of people listening. The head DJ assured me that he and his partner would not judge what I did. That put my mind at ease, although I was still unsure about what was going to happen on the phone lines.

The show went well, actually better than I expected. I was connected with three callers, interviewed in-between calls, and was out of the station before I knew it. Friends had taped the show for me and applauded me when I walked into the house. The most powerful reading I did that day was one in which a woman desired to hear from her grandmother in spirit who came through very clearly, announcing (for validation) that her birthday had just passed and that she was trying to help family members resolve a dispute over money. The call ended on a positive note with me relaying the message that a lot of heart energy and unselfishness was needed to resolve this situation. I was pleased, as I always am, to deliver such confirmation from the world of spirit to help someone. I was also happy that I had conquered new territory, breaking through my fear of going in the public eye with my mediumship. Little did I know that I would continue to shatter more previously held self-limitations in the coming year.

The Media

Soon after, I was offered the chance to do more local radio and TV shows. The segments usually consisted of a short introduction by the host, a brief interview on mediumship and psychic phenomena, followed by call-in questions. Every time I was on a show, I felt entirely blessed to be doing the work publicly, but also quite relieved when it was over. I discovered that media appearances, both radio and television, can be incredibly pressure-filled experiences. I liked the spontaneity of not knowing what callers were going to ask, but I was intensely aware of being scrutinized by the radio DJs and the public. In all fairness, not a single soul was unkind or disrespectful to me; it was merely my fear of ridicule and exposure that was causing my unease. Over time, I came to a deep realization that this mindset needed to be released. How could I expect others to value and take the work seriously if I played host to so much fear?

From the time I began professional mediumship work, I have sought to establish and maintain honesty and integrity within its scope. The true groundbreakers in modern mediumship—James Van Praagh, John Edward, Rosemary Altea, Doreen Virtue, George Anderson and others—have been able to present the concept of spirit communication in a positive light because of their genuineness. Public opinion of mediumship has changed dramatically and favorably in the past five years due largely to their efforts to bring it into the realm of respectability. In addition, the media must be credited with providing the much-needed vehicle to bring mediumship to the attention of the public. As a result, more people are shifting their beliefs to include the possibility of non-physical communication with not only departed loved ones, but spirit guides and angels as well. I believe those of us who are called to do this work must lend our voices and talents to sustain even more credibility to the reality of mediumship and its undisputed value in creating healing for those who seek it.

I am grateful for the experiences I have had in the media. It is a great privilege to be a messenger for Spirit and touch so many people who would not have been reachable without the benefit of broadcast media. When I think about the early experiences I have had in demonstrating the reality of spirit communication and other metaphysical topics through the media, I am profoundly aware that we, in our current consciousness, have touched only the tip of the iceberg, so to speak. There is so much yet to discover that will benefit the spiritual evolution of our planet.

The Creation of This Book

Some time ago, I began receiving messages from my friends and clients about writing a book as a means to share my experiences with mediumship and to teach some of the spiritual truths my guides have imparted to me. Although I felt they were right, I disregarded their suggestions because I didn't want to commit to the process of writing. Regardless of my personal resistance, the messages and feelings persisted that I needed to write. I have worked with Spirit long enough to know that if we are meant to do something, it simply *won't* go away.

The day I knew for certain I'd be writing this book was when I received a call from my father telling me that I needed to come visit him. It was two weeks before Christmas. There was something at the house for me, he said. On the way over, I had one of those gut feelings that each of us has when there is a deep sense that something important is about to happen. When I arrived, my father pulled a large box from the hall closet and announced that Santa Claus had been there already. As soon as I saw the box, I knew what it was—a new laptop computer. Three weeks before, I had casually mentioned to my parents that I was planning on buying one so that I could write a book. When my dad handed the box to me with a smile, I knew beyond a shadow of a doubt that I would write the book. The universe had made sure of it by providing the means to do it. I suspect my guides knew that I would not disappoint my father after he had thoughtfully bought me such an expensive gift!

I share this story with you to illustrate how the universe supports us when we are flowing with our purpose in life. I have seen and heard so many wonderfully compelling instances of this in the lives of my clients. The impossible suddenly and mysteriously becomes possible. As I mentioned before, at times it seems as if the very sky will open for us if what we're asking for is in accordance with our purpose in life. In the process of connecting with our purpose, we ultimately heal not only ourselves, but others. We may not be consciously aware of how we are doing it, yet we *are* doing it. If we waver in our belief and faith in ourselves, we are always miraculously led back onto the pathway that serves our divine blueprint, which is part of the overall picture in the cosmic scheme. Our intuition, the voice of the Divine within us, is our internal navigation system that guides us along the way. That is why trust in our intuition is so indispensable in the course of our life's journey. I am convinced that we also need to share our intuitive experiences with others, lest we stand alone in our newly found wisdom, no matter how great the learning.

Through my work, I have come to understand that our spirit lives on after death and that there is much more to us than our five physical senses reveal. We have the innate ability to heal ourselves through love and forgiveness that can ultimately change the world. Ties that bind us in the healing process are ties of *fear*, which keep us bound to self-limitation, and ties of *love*, which connect us to God, our loved ones in spirit, and our spiritual guides. By embracing both, we claim our full power and identity as spiritual beings. In our journey of healing, we must recognize how we have allowed fear to cloud the perception of ourselves as divine beings and then allow love to heal us. This can only be accomplished by connecting with the truth and awareness of our own spirit, which is one with God.

2

PAST PERFECT AND FUTURE PRESENT: SOUL CONTRACTS AND THE FULFILLMENT OF KARMA

At some point in our lives we have probably all heard or used the word "karma" to refer to the fortunate or unfortunate circumstances that surround us at the moment. Most people are familiar with the biblical passage that states, "As a man soweth, so shall he reap," as well as the well-worn expression, "What goes around comes around." Traditional religions teach that good actions earn positive rewards and a place in heaven, and bad or evil doings lead to punishment and a possible life in hell.

From a metaphysical perspective, karma is neither a reward system that we earn nor a form of punishment meted out by God. Simply stated, it is the universal law of cause and effect that is continuously in operation, regardless of our awareness of it. It is neither positive nor negative. It simply exists. Essentially, karma means that every thought we think, every word we speak, and every act that we do makes an imprint upon universal mind or consciousness. The frequency and vibration of our thoughts, words, and acts determine the karma that will be attached to our soul. Much like the subconscious act of breathing, we continue to create karma without conscious awareness of it. As long as we continue to take physical form, we are subject to the law of karma. As described in the chapter on past lives, reincarnation is necessary for us to balance karma and spiral toward the full realization of our divine identity.

The world of physical form serves as a schoolroom in which we learn spiritually at a faster pace than in other higher vibratory dimensions. This is due to special qualities inherent to the physical world, such as duality (good-bad, light-dark, male-female), which give us the experience of learning in polarities. Even our brains are divided into hemispheres, each one controlling diverse functions of our consciousness. Learning in duality provides opportunities for growth that occur as a result of the ultimate integration of these opposites into unity in the process of enlightenment. Only on the earth plane does this sense of separateness exist for purposes of learning.

The Akashic Records

Every thought that we have, every word we speak, and every action we take is recorded in the Akashic Records, also called the Book of Life. These records are stored in an immense library in the world of spirit as well as in our own consciousness. We may access them through meditation, past-life regression or astral travel with the permission of the Keepers of the Library, spirit beings whose duty is to guard and protect the records. Our spirit guides and Guardian Angel act as our spokespersons in gaining permission to view the records. The records are linked to our consciousness by our soul vibration and as such, are never lost from lifetime to lifetime. We continue to build and balance our records, much like a system of checks and balances until we are fully ascended into oneness or atonement (at-one-ment) with the Divine. Before coming to the earth plane in the process of birth, all memory of our past lives is blocked from our conscious awareness so that we can fully concentrate on the lifetime at hand. Upon returning to the world of spirit after death, we are once again made aware of all the aspects of our past incarnations, including the one we just left. Our Akashic Record is the source book for this review, and we usually view it in the presence of our guides who lend assistance in giving us an objective overview of our spiritual growth and direction.

Since universal law has no time limits, there is no time frame in which karma must be met. I have counseled many people with karmic patterns of emotional imbalance that originated several or many lifetimes ago that are currently being healed. The infinite wisdom of the soul, which contains the essence of God, chooses the most beneficial opportunities and circumstances available to balance karma.

Our Attitudes and Beliefs Mirror Our Karma

Included in our karma are attitudes and beliefs we hold from lifetime to lifetime. Each time we incarnate, we bring these with us into physical expression. Until we change them, we continue to attract identical or similar karmic lessons. Have you ever puzzled over some aspect of your life that continuously creates chaos, emotional pain or just plain confusion for you? Have you ever questioned why you seem to always attract the same types of social and/or romantic situations over and over? In other words, the names and faces change, but the core emotions and issues do not. This is because of the powerful magnetic quality of the thoughts, attitudes and beliefs you hold. Our thoughts create our attitudes and beliefs about everything and everyone in our life, and impact every situation we attract. Our karma mirrors our thoughts because it is a direct reflection of them.

It is important to remember that karma includes all of the good we have done in each incarnation. If a person was a great humanitarian in a particular lifetime, he carries that karma with him forever. Even if he is an average individual who accomplishes nothing special in his successive lifetime, he still carries the effects of the previous existence as a humanitarian. An example of this "carry over" is an ordinary person who has great things happen to him, such as winning millions in the lottery. Another example is one who seems to glide through life without any apparent misfortunes. These people may be viewed by society as lucky or especially blessed, when in reality they are simply experiencing the effects of "good" karma they accumulated in previous existences.

Lori, 42 and unemployed, came to me seeking guidance on both finances and relationships. While tuning into her life-force energy, I felt that she was soon going to have a small windfall come to her from a game of chance she would play. I also saw that Lori had given much time and money to others, some of which wasn't returned to her. However, much of this was about to come back to her in a lump sum directly proportional to the amount of energy she had expended. What appeared to be luck was really Lori's karma. In a subsequent session, she confirmed that she won $1,000 by playing a slot machine on a trip to Atlantic City.

The opposite can also be true in situations where a person appears to be extremely unlucky. We have all heard of individuals who have lost their life savings, been burned out of their home or experienced some other tragic circumstance. My experience of losing a business to fire served the karmic purpose of moving me into the work I do today. Although I couldn't see it at the time, the fire was a blessing because it helped connect me to my purpose. I would probably never have taken my current pathway if I had continued to operate the business. This is a good example of how karma is not always a clear-cut case in which we experience opposite or conflicting energies from one lifetime to another. Because we are constantly creating our reality, these apparent unfortunate circumstances of life occur for the ultimate growth of our soul and are very likely the result of our karmic choices on some level.

Soul Contracts

Before we come here, when we are still in our spirit bodies, we review our life lessons and what we have done in previous lifetimes. When we are contemplating coming to the physical world again, we form a contract with our parents that is mutual. They agree to be our parents and we agree to be their child for the particular karma and lessons that can be met through the experience. Please note: This does *not* mean that we consciously choose abuse, neglect, abandonment or any other painful incident of our childhood. It does mean that before we are born, we are fully aware on a soul level of what we need to both learn from and teach our parents. In the same way that we are not consciously aware of creating illness, we are often not able to fully comprehend why we have chosen to experience certain karmic patterns at any given time. That doesn't mean we aren't responsible for our lessons; it simply means that spiritual growth is seldom a cut and dried process that is easily understood with the rational mind.

From this standpoint, we cannot cloak ourselves in the identity of "victim" any longer because we have made our contracts with free will and full consent. Imagine the implications for our society if everyone remembered making these contracts and then took full responsibility for his or her own life. Among many other things, our courts of law would be virtually empty; we would stop pointing the finger at our family, friends and co-workers for "wronging" us and we would recognize our responsibility in promoting world peace. We would remember that we've chosen to live in a particular community or geographical area for the special contributions we can make in healing it. Recognition of our personal accountability for life would create a very different world than the one we live in today.

The type of contracts we make depends on the particular lessons we need to learn. If, for example, we choose to work on the lesson of forgiveness, we may form a contract with a certain person who will be in our life to help us learn it. Or we may feel a calling to do a specific task, project or career that will enable us to learn cooperation or determination. Subconsciously, we are remembering what we came here to do. Because the contracts we make are written in our soul's memory bank, they are never lost. This brings up an important question regarding purpose. How do we know exactly what we came here to do or learn?

Throughout life, we experience periodic "wake-up calls"—events, circumstances and/or relationships—that activate our awareness of the contracts we have made. Many times, the most chaotic, turbulent times in life are the ones that serve to move us to a deeper level of recognition of our life's purpose. These wake-up calls lend clues to the nature of our contracts. In order to understand these, we must view them through the eyes of higher perception. We need to remove judgment and look for the underlying theme of the experience and what it is communicating to us in terms of our spiritual growth. Although I struggled with many painful emotions, my wake-up call of recovery from alcohol abuse gave me a sublime opportunity to discover and explore my spirituality. It enabled me to get in touch with many unhealed parts of myself. It presented situations for me to speak in front of groups, which is an important component of my work today. All things considered, my recovery is a blessing.

Relationships we choose in our lives act as teaching vehicles for the expansion of our soul's growth. Our most difficult relationships can often be the greatest catalysts for us to learn about our deep-seated emotional and spiritual issues. On a soul level, each party in a relationship has agreed to learn by coming into association with one another in this way. Until the necessary lessons have been learned or the karma between the souls balanced, the association may continue from lifetime to lifetime. This type of growth takes place on a soul level and is seldom a part of our conscious awareness.

Kelly was struggling with two relationships in her life that brought her much anguish over the years. The first of these was her relationship with her father, an emotionally cold and controlling man who had never given Kelly the unconditional love and support she needed while growing up. Besides feeling as if she had lived in the shadow of his domineering personality most of her life, Kelly never felt validated as a woman. Strict Irish Catholics, her family tended to give more respectability to the male members of the clan. As a result, Kelly felt as if she really did not amount to much in the eyes of her family.

Interestingly, Kelly married a man much like her father. Her husband Nick had the same callous attitude toward her and was often reluctant to show her any affection. He was unsympathetic to Kelly's wants, needs, and life ambitions, which included an innate ability to draw and paint. From childhood on, Kelly had been unable to express herself to her family and husband. When she did, she was either put down or ignored. Artwork was the only channel of expression in which she felt safe enough to allow her soul to speak. During both sessions I had with her, I saw how Kelly had chosen to learn about claiming her own power through both her family and her marriage. It was very apparent that she had karmic ties and contracts with both her father and her husband.

Due to the stress of living inauthentically, Kelly developed a heart condition that caused her much anxiety. I could see clairvoyantly how her heart chakra (the energy center of love) had energetically narrowed in response to her emotions of distrust and the emotional pain she had suffered. It was also clear that Kelly needed to release the karma attached to these two relationships in which she had learned so much about asserting her own power. Although she is not ready to completely detach from them, Kelly has experienced some awareness about what all of this has been teaching her. I suggested she work on releasing as much fear of her self-expression as she could through her artwork. To reestablish her level of trust in relating to others, I suggested she join a group where she feels secure enough to express herself.

This is one example of the type of contract we can make in order to learn. There are many others, each one offering its own unique set of opportunities for us to stretch our spiritual boundaries. The amount of time it takes us to complete our contracts is dependent on the particular lessons we have come to address. Some souls come to earth for only a short period of time in order to serve as a teacher for their parents or others—such as infants and children who are born with or develop life-threatening illnesses. Other souls come to volunteer to advance medical science in one form or another through having a particular illness. Through the experience of doing so, they not only help humanity but also advance themselves spiritually.

The spectrum of contracts that we have to choose from is as rich and colorful as the tapestries of our souls. There may be many situations where we don't understand what agreement has been made between two individuals. As stated earlier, it is important that we remove judgment as much as possible and simply trust that spiritual learning is taking place through *every* contract. We are fortunate indeed if we come to understand our own lessons, much less the lessons of someone else.

What happens if we do not complete our contracts in one lifetime? Upon return to the spirit world, we review and make plans to continue our lessons on the Other Side, or in a future incarnation. Again we will choose optimal time, place and conditions that benefit our growth. Until we are ready to return to earth, we rest, study, play, contemplate our spiritual lessons, or facilitate healing for loved ones who remain in the physical world.

Like Attracts Like or Why am I Having Such a Hard Time in the Relationships of Life?

In addition to the law of karma, the *universal law of resonance* is always in operation and, much like karma, acts independently from our awareness of it. Simply stated, it is the principle that similar or identical energies attract one another. An example of this is being in a crowded room yet managing to find another individual who resonates with us on some level of our consciousness. Sometimes this is a magnetism that emanates from an unhealed part of us. Some people who have come to me for readings have said that they have had magnetic attractions to people who they believed to be their soulmate, only to discover that the person to whom they were attracted had become the antithesis of their dream lover. They invariably ask the question, "Why am I in this relationship?" Many times, we will unconsciously attract to us people who are mirroring our own unresolved issues from past lives and childhood. Conflicts arise in relationships when we are facing our own thoughts, attitudes and beliefs that need confronted and healed. The origin of the conflict lies in our resistance to releasing fear-based patterns that no longer serve us.

We can just as easily attract others who mirror our divine attributes—such as unconditional love, compassion and forgiveness. This usually occurs after we have healed ourselves enough to allow the light of our soul to shine without clouds of fear blocking it. We release thoughts such as, "I don't feel complete without being in a relationship," and replace them with ones that affirm our wholeness such as, "I am perfect in myself." Instead of attracting from a state of *lack*, we attract from one of *abundance*. This shift in our perception makes a striking difference in our ability to attract healthy, loving relationships. When we fully realize that we are complete within ourselves, we freely attract others who share this perception. We invite others to accompany us in relationship for the mutual joy of self-discovery.

Transitions and Healing in Spiritual Growth

During spiritual transformation, we usually enter into what is an introspective period of self-examination that is precipitated by feelings of unrest. This is a period of intense soul searching, confusion, or depression that often precedes a major breakthrough in our consciousness. We may feel temporarily disconnected from, disillusioned with, and isolated from family and friends, our jobs and society. Physical illness may be a factor as well. Many people experience feelings of discontent, restlessness and chaos. These experiences indicate that we are about to make some sort of major transition in our lives. The earth beneath our feet may feel unfamiliar and shaky as we ride the storm of uncertainty that has temporarily cast darkness on our lives. I use the word "temporarily" because all spiritual and emotional shifts, no matter how seemingly insurmountable at the time, eventually pass and give way to restoration of equilibrium within our souls. Many 12-step recovery programs use a slogan that gives hope to members who experience the confusing feelings that accompany spiritual growth—"This too shall pass." We have created the so-called dramas and traumas of life so we can effectively move beyond self-imposed limitations and function at higher levels of spiritual consciousness.

There are many events in life that may precipitate a shift within our consciousness and a subsequent release and/or healing of our karmic patterns. These include marriage, divorce, the birth of a child, illness, the passing of a loved one, a career change or unemployment. When we afford ourselves the opportunity to view our particular circumstances with the spiritual eye of intuitive insight, we can process the transformation we are making much more rapidly and easily. This process necessitates a period of inner reflection in order to gain insight. The amount of emotional pain and difficulty we experience in adjusting to transition is directly proportional to the amount of resistance we have to seeing the spiritual lesson in a situation. The key to transition and release of karmic patterns is the use of our intuitive insight to guide us into *flow*, which is the release of resistance. Here are three crucial questions to ask in the midst of transition:

1. Why have I attracted this lesson (person, situation, event) to me?
2. What have I learned from this?
3. How can I release it?

The answers to these questions should be written down in a personal journal where you can record your innermost thoughts and feelings. Judgment—that can take the form of being critical of others and/or ourselves—can be a huge block to the understanding of spiritual lessons. It is important that you write down the first impressions you receive in response to the above questions without the filter of judgment. A brief meditation prior to writing is often beneficial to the process of exploring your thoughts and feelings.

Once you have asked for guidance on these questions and written the responses, ask for intuitive awareness in understanding the lessons inherent in your circumstances. Perhaps you are in the process of releasing a relationship that no longer fulfills you. Upon examining your response to the questions of why you have attracted it, you may discover a pattern you have held in previous relationships. These patterns are indicators of blockages you hold from both childhood and past life experiences. When you recognize them, you can begin to heal them.

The release of emotional blockages can occur quickly or slowly, depending upon our level of resistance to recognizing, understanding and letting them go. Sometimes we have held the patterns for many lifetimes and they have become quite comfortable, however dysfunctional they may be. Unfortunately, many people are reluctant to confront their life issues unless faced with major life trauma such as illness, divorce or unemployment. They are unaware that they have choice and opportunity to release karma and heal at any time. We can learn through joy just as easily as through personal crisis. Most of the time, though, we need to experience change through direct confrontation with our unhealed thoughts and emotions.

Because we have all lived multiple lifetimes, we have built layers of karma around our soul. Taking physical form gives us the opportunity to release these layers in stages and become one with God, which is called *ascension*. After we ascend, there is no need to return to the earth plane because we have mastered its lessons. Jesus, Buddha, Krishna and the Ascended Masters are examples of souls who have released all karmic lessons and earthly incarnations. They are the most highly evolved souls that have lived in the physical world and serve as models for the process of enlightenment for humankind. Because they have successfully released all human limitations and exist universally, we may call on any or all of these masters in our own journey toward enlightenment. They are always available to inspire and heal us.

Karmic blockages may be released through different methods. After we become aware of them, we can ask for help in releasing them through meditation and prayer, both of which directly connect us with the healing energy of God. Past-life regression is also a valuable tool in understanding and releasing karma because it provides the means to uncover the origin of a pattern and then heal it. Hands-on healing techniques—such as Reiki and spiritual healing—are energy-based and tend to bypass the layers and resistance of the conscious mind, which allows for deeper release. When I perform spiritual healings, I pray for the highest and best healing that the individual is able to accept. I've discovered that the deepest healings occur when we release our expectations and simply open our hearts to receive what we need.

What happens if we choose to remain in denial of our unhealed karma? We *compound* our karma, which means we add layers of similar unbalanced thoughts to the ones that presently exist in our consciousness. Ultimately, we must face and heal all of our karma, in this lifetime or successive ones. The sooner we heal ourselves, the better.

As human consciousness shifts and continues to evolve toward a higher vibration, we are becoming increasingly aware of the need to explore and heal the "wounds" of our past. We are coming to the realization that we alone are responsible for the direction and quality of our lives. We are discovering that the greatest and most profound journey is the one we take on the pathway that leads to an incredible and breath-taking destination. It is the realization of our soul's divine and sacred identity.

KEEPING A SPIRITUAL JOURNAL

Through my experience of teaching spiritual and intuitive development, I have discovered that it is most helpful to maintain a journal that can be used for recording one's thoughts, words, and feelings. Journaling serves two purposes: First, writing down what is experienced during meditation creates a more concrete validation of the mental, emotional, and spiritual processes that occur during altered states of consciousness. The significance of symbolism, visual imagery, and key themes may be forgotten if not recorded. This is necessary in gaining a deeper and more expansive understanding of self. Secondly, journaling enables you to keep a logbook of valuable insights obtained over an indefinite period of time. You can reflect on these writings for further insight and wisdom in the process of spiritual development. Simply put, patterns of growth can be more easily recognized when they are recorded in writing. For these reasons, I recommend that you keep a "spiritual" journal when reading this book, especially when doing the self-enlightenment exercises and questions at the end of each chapter.

Many of the questions and exercises are designed to stimulate your thoughts and feelings about particular subjects as they relate to your spiritual awareness, which is a reflection of your own personal experiences of life. As such, there are no right or wrong answers to the questions, or "correct" ways to do the exercises. I recommend that you approach each set of exercises with an open mind, and most importantly, an open heart, towards your soul's unique journey through life.

Questions and Exercises for Self-Enlightenment

1. What are some of the attitudes and beliefs you currently hold? Have you felt these from a young age? Try to examine all areas of your life, including the spiritual, mental, emotional and physical. In your journal, on the left-hand side of a page, make a list of them.

2. Next, think of some repetitive patterns you have experienced in your life. These can include the patterns you have experienced within interpersonal relationships, career choices, family and health. List these on the right side of the same page as above. Now look at both lists and see how the two interrelate. How might your attitudes and beliefs be reflective of the patterns you have seen in your life? Are they direct mirrors? Write a sentence or two on what this correlation is telling you about your karmic tendencies.

3. Take a few moments to do a quick review of your life. What contracts do you feel you have made before coming here? A good clue to this is how you feel about particular areas of your life. Look for patterns. Did you come to learn a certain quality such as nurturing? In the relationships of your life, are there special people with whom you feel bonded? Who have been the "teachers" in your life and what have they taught you about yourself?

4. Again think of your life until the present moment. What wake-up calls have occurred? How did they act as catalysts for your personal transformation? How might your life be different today if they had not occurred?

5. Think of a particularly painful relationship, event or circumstance you have experienced. Ask yourself

the three questions relating to transition in this chapter. View the situation without judgment. What new insights does this give you on why you have experienced this? How have you grown spiritually as a result of going through it? Journal your answers.

3

Our Past Lives and How They Affect Us Today

The concept of the eternal nature of the soul is an ancient one. From early recorded history until the present day, mankind has believed in the concept of the indestructibility of the human soul after physical death. An example of this can be found in the religious systems of the ancient Egyptians who believed the soul journeyed to the underworld after physical death in continuation of its learning experience. As children growing up in a predominantly Christian nation, most of us were taught about the concept of heaven and the blessings that await us there, where we would commune with angels and live in eternal peace. We were also warned of the possibility of spending eternity in hell if we failed to obey the word of God and adhere to particular religious teachings. The idea that we come back to the earth in another body to continue our spiritual growth was seldom, if ever, mentioned. We were taught we have only one life to learn all we need to know about God and ourselves.

Eastern religions such as Buddhism and Hinduism teach a different concept of the soul's journey. In these systems of thought each soul incarnates again and again until the ultimate process of enlightenment and union with the Divine occurs. There are no limits to the number of lifetimes a soul may experience. Each incarnation is necessary for the purposes of learning about the divine nature of soul and to balance karma. All the experiences that we have in any given lifetime are recorded in the Akashic Record or Book of Life, which is the sum total of all of our thoughts, words and deeds from the time of our soul's origin. No experience is lost from our records, even if it is transmuted by our conscious or subconscious release of the karma attached to it. Upon incarnation, all memory of prior existence is veiled from our conscious mind. This serves the purpose of allowing the incarnating soul to focus exclusively on the present lifetime. When we return to the spirit world after death, we are once again given full knowledge contained in our records.

Many people have *déjà vu*, the sensation of remembering similar experiences from prior time. These are "triggers," or automatic recalls, that provide remembrance of the soul's prior experiences. How many of us have met a person, visited a place, or been in a social situation that seems hauntingly familiar to us in some way? Most of us can recall having these types of unexplained occurrences. It is because we are remembering at a very deep level our past associations with the same souls, places or experiences. We have no rational explanation for these occurrences despite the familiarity of the feelings they evoke within us, because conscious memories of the past association have been blocked from our recollection. However, the soul remembers the imprint of the energy, and that is what causes us to experience a tinge of recognition.

The concepts of reincarnation, karma and the continuity of life are often depicted in the symbol of the wheel. In the Hindu tradition, it represents the cycle of death and rebirth that we are destined to repeat until we no longer need the lessons that physical existence provides. The wheel is also a representation of the circle, which traditionally signifies unity, order and completion. Each time we take form in a physical body, we prepare for a lifetime of learning that will enable us to move closer to the full realization of our divine nature. It is important to remember that there is no concept of time in the eternal essence of our souls. An entire life span of perhaps 80 years may be spent on understanding and developing a single soul quality such as patience or forgiveness. On the other hand, it may take us several or multiple lifetimes to develop it. It is entirely dependent upon our willingness to release our limitations of who we think we are, change our beliefs, and fully embrace our sacred identity.

Why We Choose to Come Here

Interestingly, although there is no concept of time on a soul level for lessons to be learned, the very nature of the earth plane—with the elements of time and space—afford us the ability to learn at a faster pace if we so choose. How is this so? When we take physical form, we are better able to experience and incorporate the lessons we need. The vibrations of the earth are relatively dense and slow compared to the higher planes of Spirit where there is no time, space or form. Being in physical form slows things down for us so we are better able to learn. It is like watching instant replay in a televised sports game. When the picture is slowed down, we are often able to see exactly what occurred, where a player may have fumbled, and the specific mechanics of the entire play. On the physical plane we have the advantage and luxury of time, which enables us to think before we act or see the results of our thoughts in physical form. This is not so in the higher dimensions where time does not exist. There, thought manifests instantly.

One of my teachers illustrated this concept with the following example: To understand the difference in the vibration of the earth plane versus the higher ones, think of a man who is planning to rob a bank. If he is in physical form, he takes stock of his options for choosing the bank he'll rob, executing the robbery and making a hasty getaway. He may even plan what he is going to do with the money once he has stolen it. In between his planning and the actual robbery lies the element of time. He is afforded the opportunity to change his mind and perhaps even become a law-abiding citizen. In contrast, if this same man exists in the astral or fourth dimension, the *second* he thinks of robbing the bank, he has robbed it.

This example also illustrates the point that our thoughts define our reality. Whether we are in physical or spiritual form, the determining factor in the creation of all of experiences is the vibration of our thoughts. The precious value of the element of time in a spiritual sense, is the ability it gives us to use our free will to *choose* and evaluate our choices.

Taking physical form enables us to experience growth that can happen in no other way. In addition to having the opportunity to balance karma from past incarnations, we are given the vehicle of the physical body through which we can learn spiritual lessons. The expression of our soul in physical form is a reflection of the many and varied karmic patterns we have come here to address. Each cell and atom of the body contains the vibration of our soul's consciousness, which is the sum total of all its experiences. In essence, we are nothing more or nothing less than the thoughts we have expressed or are expressing. The more closely those thoughts resonate with the perfection of God, the less karma we create each time we come into physical reality. This is accomplished by aligning our will with God's will.

How and Why We Choose Time, Place, and Circumstances in Coming Here

All of us have led a plethora of lifetimes, incarnating in the optimal time and in the circumstances most conducive to our soul's growth. Some people who have come to me for past-life readings ask, "Why would I choose to be born into a family who used, abused, neglected or abandoned me?" My answer is: you *wouldn't* have chosen it on a personality level. However, on a soul level you chose your family and they chose you because each of you was the best teacher for your soul's purpose and advancement at the time. It is impossible to understand the workings of the soul when one is looking through the eyes of the ego or personality. These are functions of our earthly minds, which will never be able to fully comprehend the mystery and majesty of the soul. We must learn to speak to our soul on its own terms and in its own language, which is much grander than we can fathom with our earthly perspective. It is language that is contained not in words, but in feelings that connect us in the absolute moment with all of creation—past, present, and future.

The particular circumstances of our incarnation are primarily determined by the karma we need to meet and balance. As mentioned before, karma is neither positive nor negative; it simply exists. The fact that it determines the conditions of each incarnation means that it influences our choice of birth family, nationality, culture, class consciousness, genetic coding, and any other circumstances we may require for our soul's growth. We choose each of these based on the unique needs of our soul. The following is an example of how we choose to balance and heal karma by experiencing specific earthly settings that allow us to redefine and stretch our spiritual boundaries.

James, 48, is a man with a long history of abuse and addiction issues. As a child, John was both sexually and emotionally abused by his stepfather, an alcoholic. Over the years that he lived at home, he learned to adapt to the regular molestations and beatings that were nearly a daily routine. When John turned 18, he joined the military and immediately began drinking and using cocaine to escape the pain of his childhood. He was arrested and spent time in a military prison for selling drugs. When he was released, he decided to enter a treatment program for addiction. He also sought counseling for the years of abuse he suffered while growing up.

Over time, John came to realize that he has struggled with the issue of understanding his personal power. Interestingly, when he was regressed in a past life session, he recalled a lifetime in which he was a Roman soldier who had tortured and imprisoned many people. Because this was his "duty" as a military soldier, he never felt remorse or guilt for what he had done. Regardless of his lack of feelings, the traumatic emotional imprint of that lifetime was recorded in John's Book of Life. Because of this, John incarnated in his present life with the karma of the Roman lifetime unresolved. In the regression, John recognized his stepfather as one of the prisoners he tortured. To spiritually balance what he had done, John chose to experience the same issues of power and control from the opposite perspective. Like most of us, he also chose to incarnate with some of the same souls, because the scales had been left unbalanced in those relationships.

It is important to note that not all of the spiritual lessons we come here to learn are as clear-cut as John's. There are many factors affecting the karma we create and fulfill. We do not always experience opposite energies from lifetime to lifetime. Rather, the nature and extent of our lessons and growth depend on the intricate workings of the soul in its perfection. In addition, we may wait many lifetimes to balance karma that was created earlier. We carry the imprint of the karmic experience with us from the moment it is formed. How and when we balance it is dependent on the choices we make. One thing is certain, however: we come here in the perfect time and circumstances that will further what we need to learn on a spiritual level.

Trust is the one essential element that we need in our approach to understanding and healing our karmic patterns.

Because trust is accomplished through opening our hearts to God and our highest good at all times, it becomes necessary for us to approach the healing of karma through unconditional love and forgiveness. In fact, the only way to release the chains that have bound us to the past is to make passage through the compassion of our heart centers. It is no coincidence that the heart center is the mediator between the lower and the upper chakras. When we balance all energies through the gateway of the heart, we have closed the chasm between our egos and our God selves, enabling release and forgiveness. This is an essential part of our healing journey.

Karmic Relationships

One of the areas of greatest concern for people in relation to past lives is the subject of relationships. Often people come for intuitive counseling when they feel stuck or overwhelmed with issues in one of their primary relationships. Frequently, they experience an inability to move forward because of their resistance to releasing old patterns, which often have their origins in past lives with the same souls they are currently with. When past lives are revealed, it is often discovered that the previous relationship has set the stage, so to speak, for the current one in terms of emotional blockages. The essential nature of *all* relationships in our lives is one of personal reflection, introspection and healing. In this way all of our associations with others—whether they are romantic, familial or business—mirror aspects of ourselves.

Relationships exist because we learn best through interactions with other souls. Because of the universal law of like energy attracting like energy, we can use the lessons being reflected to us in our close ties to learn about our emotional imbalances and spiritual lessons. From lifetime to lifetime, we may reincarnate with the same group of souls but in different roles and genders. For example, a soul who may have been our mother in one incarnation may reincarnate and associate with us as our child in order to balance karma and advance spiritually. Similarly, our husband from a previous life may be our brother or sister in current day. This readjustment is necessary for each soul's advancement. In many instances, the core of the lessons remains the same. The difference is that we are able to experience the lesson from a different perspective, which provides us with greater opportunity for integration of it.

The subject of soulmates has been widely discussed in many popular metaphysical books. Although beliefs vary, many people still think their soulmate is one who is their true heart's desire and companion. Although this can be the case, this definition is limiting because it does not take into account many situations in which our soulmate is someone who acts as a powerful catalyst for our spiritual growth. He or she is our greatest teacher in one or more lifetimes, reflecting to us our deepest fears, insecurities and lessons that need to be examined and healed. This does not mean that we are destined to ride off into the sunset with this individual. A soulmate may be an abusive parent or spouse, a domineering or controlling teacher or a tyrannical employer who takes advantage of us. Any one of these relationships could act as compelling agents for personal transformation if we choose, and any of these people could be our soulmate. It is possible to have more than one soulmate in a single lifetime, depending on the unique needs of our soul. We may spend years with one individual to gather the experiences we require and then enter into relationship with another to further our growth. These arrangements are made prior to our coming here when we are in the spirit world.

We choose to experience relationships to learn about ourselves in various ways that could never occur if we were to remain alone. The mirroring aspects that relationships provide in the context of our spiritual growth are significant and lasting. Just as mirrors reflect our physical appearance, relationships mirror the emotional and spiritual issues of our consciousness. They may bring up our deepest and most fear-based thought patterns. They may cause us to examine unhealed parts of our emotions that need to surface and be released. Or, they may bring us great feelings of joy, union, harmony, and love. In either case, relationships are always a contractual arrangement between two or more souls for purposes of growth.

Dreams, Affinities and Other Clues to Past Lives

Sometimes we may experience what I call a "bleedthrough" of past lives, which means that we become consciously aware of one or more of our past incarnations. In addition to *déjà vu*, this may occur in the dream state when the subconscious mind is most active. Some people experience flashbacks of settings, episodes or people from earlier times. They may even see themselves in a different persona. It is not entirely clear why this occurs, but I believe it comes about as a result of our subconscious mind linking similar patterns of feeling and experience in an attempt to sort them out. For example, if a person is currently dealing with emotional issues of claiming personal power, she may subconsciously recall past experiences where she confronted the same issues. Another example would be an individual who dreams of another time and place in which she was involved in relationship with a person who is present in her life today. In this instance, there is a deep soul recognition that takes place despite obvious physical differences.

In the soul, past, present, and future are one and time doesn't exist. Because of this, we can access any experience we've had through our subconscious mind. The "past" still exists in all its detail and we may "time travel" there during sleep or during altered states of consciousness. It is much to our advantage to record and interpret the past life associations we become aware of. They not only provide clues to who and where we have been, but may shed light on karmic patterns that need to be healed.

Some metaphysicians speculate that it is possible to "travel" to the future. Since the soul exists independently of time and space, it can exist in many realities simultaneously. During the dream state, we may visit probable scenarios that can come about as a result of our current choices. We are experiencing our lives before we actually live them in a physical sense. Free will gives us the opportunity to change our lives at any point. Much research has yet to be done on the subject of "future" lives.

The particular likes and dislikes we have for food, clothing, artwork, architecture, music and places are clues that reveal our past lives. I have seen many examples of this in readings I have done for people.

Helen came for intuitive sessions because she was intensely interested in uncovering who she had been in previous incarnations. During the second session, I clearly saw her as a wealthy young woman in 18th century France. A scene came forth of her playing a harpsichord in an ornate drawing room decorated in gold with beautiful pieces of artwork on the walls. There were many shelves of books nearby that seemed to be part of an extensive library. Helen immediately connected with this scene when she shared that she has always loved harpsichord music and is a voluminous reader. Further, she stated that she had majored in art history in college. In addition, she was able to strongly identify with the emotional patterning of that lifetime, in which she had valued safety and security in her father's household to the exclusion of anything else.

Another observation I have made from doing intuitive sessions with people is their affinity for certain cultures, ethnic groups and countries without apparent reason. The first time

I met Jamie, 47, I was immediately struck by her physical appearance. With long, shiny hair and dark eyes, she reminded me of a Native American princess. When I began speaking to her, I sensed that she had a deep resonance with healing energies, particularly those emanating from natural sources such as the earth. I could clairvoyantly see a lifetime in which Jamie had been a Native American who worked as a healer in her tribe. I saw her close identification with herbal remedies that were used to treat various ailments. Jamie later shared that she had always been attracted to Native American culture since she was a small child. In the last ten years she became interested in and studied herbal medicine and holistic healing. She also does Native American totem animal readings for people, an experience she finds very enlightening and rewarding. Clearly, Jamie's prior experiences as a Native healer continue to impact her current life choices.

Many other individuals I've met are at a loss to provide a logical explanation for their current inclinations towards a particular career pathway, geographical location or area of study. Many feel drawn to a certain area of the country, but are not sure why they feel a desire to visit or settle there. During sessions with them, it is often revealed that they once inhabited the same area in a prior incarnation. I have known this to be the case with individuals who have unfinished business with a soul group (souls who share a similar purpose) or other former associations from an area that they feel "called" to visit. Other individuals have had a relatively pleasant and peaceful existence in a location and simply desire to return to it. Some have karmic attachment to certain land or property, which they have agreed to own, protect or develop in some way, based on prior karmic contractual agreement.

Keep in mind that we cannot always categorize and simplify the spiritual lessons we face. The complex nature of the soul defies rational explanation, which arranges things in neat packages for the benefit of the ego. The value of understanding past lives lies mainly in the healing that takes place once we are aware of karmic emotional patterns, tendencies, and relationships. Since the initial step in healing is awareness, knowledge of who and where we have been can be of primary importance in making assessment of what we need to heal. However, we must remember to not allow ourselves to seek escape in the nostalgia, glamour or pain of our pasts. That defeats the purpose of bringing the past to the surface. As with everything in our lives, examination of the past needs to be approached from a balanced perspective. By doing so, we can gain new insights into the depths of our being.

The Eternal Nature of the Soul

The most important point to keep in mind when considering reincarnation and past lives is the eternal nature of the soul and its continual evolution. In addition to the wheel, the symbol of the *spiral* depicts the concept of the soul's journey through many and varied incarnations. Each circle in the spiral may represent many lifetimes at a similar level until we are ready to move to the next circle, or level of consciousness. On each individual journey or lifetime, we experience and embrace similar or diverse circumstances, depending upon our purpose or intent for that lifetime. Before taking physical form, we discuss the status of our lessons with our spiritual teachers and guides. We are afforded the opportunity to see, in full panoramic vision, the "movie" of any given lifetime we are contemplating. During this process, we are shown the probable circumstances of each lifetime and their implications for our spiritual advancement. This is the point at which we make karmic agreements that will serve to further our growth and the growth of others. Based on what we need to learn, we choose the circumstances of our incarnation that will best meet our needs. Ultimately, because of free will, the responsibility for the spiritual progression of our soul lies with us and only us. No one—including our guides, angels and spiritual masters—can interfere with our free will. Therefore, the contracts we make prior to incarnation are always by our own design and volition.

Learning does not stop in between physical lifetimes. We continue to progress in the worlds of spirit where form does not exist. The length of time between incarnations is determined by the specific needs of the soul. Some souls may choose to reincarnate immediately to continue a cycle of growth. Others may rest for extended periods in the quiet and concentrated healing found in spirit hospitals in the spirit world. This seems to be true for those who have experienced a long, debilitating illness (such as AIDS or cancer) while on earth. These decisions are usually made upon review of the lifetime just completed when a person makes transition to the world of spirit. After passage through the tunnel of light, we are shown all the details, circumstances and mission of the life we have led. Then we confer with our spiritual guides, who assist us in understanding the implications of what we have experienced. They help us to make the best decisions concerning our future growth. We then continue in the manner best suited to us.

Suicide

A word needs to be said about suicide as it applies to reincarnation. Despite the eternal nature of the soul, the taking of one's life short-circuits one's own growth, and causes devastating emotional pain and grief for loved ones. Ultimately we are the only judge and jury in the courtroom of our lives. From this perspective, suicide is not a morally wrong choice, but one that defeats and delays our spiritual progress and growth. We must deal with healing painful emotional issues either here in the physical plane, or in the world of spirit. One who commits suicide finds himself in the same bewildering and painful emotional state as he was before crossing over. There is always help available from compassionate spirit beings who offer healing to those who ask for it. The individual's spirit guides are available to assist him in understanding and evaluating the choices he made in life. He may be shown options based on the decisions he's made and counseled about the best pathway to take to heal emotionally. This may include the opportunity to facilitate healing from the spirit world for those on earth who have experienced the loss of a loved one through suicide. Or he can take physical form again immediately to finish the life he left. Finally, he can rest for a period of time in the spirit world and further review his life. In any case, he must face and take final responsibility for his choices and actions.

In sessions where a loved one comes through who has committed suicide, strong messages of regret are usually communicated. Often, these spirits speak of their emotional and mental confusion before passing and express feelings of sadness for causing pain to the family. After passing into the spirit world, these spirits are able to see the larger picture of their lives and the options they neglected to consider before taking their own lives.

Nicky, 34, lost her husband, Bob, an alcoholic, to suicide. When Bob came through, he told her he was finally getting the help he needed in a rehabilitation center in the spirit world. "He was not able to do that when he was alive," Nicky sobbed softly. "He was too stubborn to seek help." Bob also communicated that he was sorry for leaving in the way he did because it had caused so much grief for the family and that he had not done his part in being a good husband or father. "I'm looking out for you now," he said. "I didn't do a very good job of that when I was on earth."

For people who have lost a loved one to suicide, I highly recommend attending individual grief counseling sessions and bereavement groups. It is extremely beneficial in the healing process to share your feelings with others who have similar experiences and are sensitive to your feelings. The American Suicide Foundation (800-531-4477) offers resources for suicide prevention and survivors of suicide. Other local organizations and services can be located in your phone directory under the general category of "Mental Health."

Questions and Exercises for Self-Enlightenment

1. Think about the times and circumstances in which you experienced *déjà vu*. Does there seem to be a pattern to these occurrences? Have you felt drawn to a particular field of study, time period or country? What could this be revealing to you?

2. Take a moment to examine the nature and quality of the relationships in your life. Has there been a particular role you have played within your family of origin? Do you find yourself in the same role in other circumstances of your life? Look for and identify emotional patterns of your life. What are these showing you about yourself?

3. Is there someone in your life with whom you feel a special bond or particular dislike? In what ways do you feel you have been connected with this person before? What have you learned about yourself from the relationship?

4. Keep a dream journal in which you record significant dreams. Make special note of any dreams that contain unfamiliar settings, countries, languages, and/ or clothing. What clues do these provide for you regarding past lives?

5. If you could experience a certain life or set of circumstances, what would they be? List ways in which this speaks to you of your soul mission, lessons and emotional patterns. How are you presently incorporating aspects of the life you dream of into your present situation? Compare and contrast the two.

4

BOUND TO UNIVERSAL LAW: THE ROLE OF KARMA IN PHYSICAL AND EMOTIONAL HEALING

The primary focus of my work as a spiritual medium and intuitive counselor has been to act as a support for people who are seeking healing of some sort. The bulk of my work is done through private readings in which I offer guidance, direction and confirmation in many areas of my clients' lives. In my practice, I have met people from many different walks of life—including occupation, social class, and culture. As unique as each may be, most of them have one thing in common: they are seeking to heal and move beyond wounds of the past that have become too painful and limiting for them to carry any longer. Although they may have come to the session from very different backgrounds and situations, each individual is basically searching for guidance on how to live a more fulfilling and harmonious life. In essence, they are opening their awareness to release what is not working in their lives anymore and to incorporate new avenues of balance and wholeness into their existence.

Among the many insights I have obtained through my work, one of the most profound has been that all emotional and physical healing originates from within the individual. There is nothing anyone can do to *make* us heal. We must have the willingness to want to change and release the imbalance in our thinking that created the illness or disease. We must then implement the changes that are necessary for healing to occur. Until we do so, we are merely on the treadmill of masking symptoms, and not really examining the root causes of emotional distress, illness and disease. Even when a condition appears to go away, if it has not been addressed from a core level, it will almost always reappear, either identical to its original form or in another form.

The Meaning of Healing

What does it mean to heal? Simply, it is a return to the state of balance and harmony in one's life-force energy. It also means clearing the chakra system(See Part 2) of unbalanced thoughts and emotions to permit the free flow of this vital life-force. We make daily choices regarding the distribution of our life-force energy. Because of the law of karma, our previous choices always affect our present ones. Most people use their past experiences as determining factors in making present or future choices. Blockages in the chakras occur when we hold onto and allow fear-based emotional responses to disrupt the natural flow of life-force energy through these centers. Fear-based emotions originate from our ego center and restrict our ability to be in our divine power, which is love. (Examples of these emotions are anger, resentment, jealousy, power and control issues, hatred and generalized fear of life.) Such emotions have the tendency to "freeze' or slow our life energy and keep us locked into the limitation of the ego, which always views things—including our own nature and experiences—in separate, restrictive terms. Eventually, we are faced with the unavoidable consequences of holding these patterns of thought and must begin to either heal them or repeat the process of learning, usually in a more intense manner.

Although healing can occur through many different treatment methods, the common denominator is changing the thought patterns that created the imbalance in the beginning. If our thoughts are not changed at this fundamental level, healing will not occur. This does not mean that a person will not recover from an illness or that symptoms will not disappear. It *does* mean that unless the thought that caused the imbalance to manifest is released, he is prone to creating the same or a similar condition. This may occur in a single lifetime, or many incarnations, in which the same thoughts are carried forward until they are released and ultimately healed.

Karmic Illnesses and the Physical Body

For purposes of review, karma means the law of cause and effect. We reap what we sow. This includes all of our thoughts, words and actions in any given lifetime and even in between them, when we are in the world of spirit. Because of the immortality of the soul, the process of spiritual learning and growth is infinite. When we transition from the physical body, our journey of self-understanding and enlightenment continues in other dimensions. We may choose to immediately return to the earth plane or further our growth in dimensions where we exist without form, depending upon what our mission and lessons are at any given time. One thing for certain, however, is that we must meet and balance our soul's karma in order to advance spiritually. One of the vehicles that enables us to do this is the physical body.

Our body is a reflection of all of the thoughts that we are

holding. Quite simply, we are nothing more nor less than our thoughts allow us to be. This includes the storehouse of all of the experiences we have had in previous incarnations, as well as in our current lifetime. Before coming to the physical plane, when in spirit, we review the lessons that we will be coming to understand and heal while in physical form. Our spirit guides, angels and teachers assist us in preparing to take these steps. They help us to review where we have been and what we still need to accomplish. However, we always have the final decision in exactly how and when we learn those lessons. Our guides help us to view our lessons from a detached frame of reference, and provide guidance on the best manner in which we can proceed.

Sometimes we may choose to balance our karma through experiencing a physical condition such as an illness or physical limitation. Other times, we may have been unwilling or unable to heal an emotional imbalance in a previous lifetime and may choose to try again. Because of the particular circumstances that having a physical body presents, especially when it comes to illness, we may choose to meet our karma by experiencing it in the body. The physical plane is the last opportunity that we have to balance and heal karmic obligation because it is the lowest vibratory plane of our soul's existence. We continue to meet and balance karma in between incarnations, although not as easily. There is no time factor involved due to the eternal nature of the soul. A soul may take many hundreds of years to meet one aspect of karma. The readings of Edgar Cayce, the great clairvoyant trance healer, are full of examples of souls who incarnated again and again to balance and meet the same karmic responsibilities (see *Edgar Cayce on Reincarnation* by Noel Langley, Warner Books, 1967; and *Edgar Cayce's Story of Attitudes and Emotions*, ed. by Jeffrey Furst, Berkley Books, 1976).

I have counseled people who are presently meeting unhealed karma from prior incarnations. Fran, a woman in her late thirties, suffered from severe attacks of asthma. She was also claustrophobic and sometimes afraid to stay in her home. These attacks would occur when she was undergoing periods of emotional stress and were particularly related to times when she felt threatened by her family—especially her older sister, who was very controlling. Whenever Fran had an attack, she felt as if she could not breathe and had to leave her house. Through successive intuitive sessions with her, I was able to see that once Fran had suffocated in a cave that was covered from a landfall; she and her family at the time were unable to escape. The experience made such a traumatic imprint on Fran's emotional psyche that she had carried the fear into her present incarnation in physical and emotional imbalances. Because of the relative trauma and suddenness of her death in that lifetime, she felt a loss of control in most areas of her life and often allowed others to control her emotionally. Her thoughts went something like, "I cannot be responsible for my own life so others must do that for me." As a result, Fran had several deeply painful relationships with men who were manipulative and who tended to be overly critical of her. She hadn't been able to successfully find and keep a job, drifting from place to place. I suggested past-life regression therapy as a healing tool to help her release the thoughtforms that kept her feeling so imprisoned in her life. Intuitively, I sensed she was currently too fearful to take this crucial step in the healing process. The last I heard from Fran, she was still attempting to heal her emotions from the events that happened so long ago.

We can and do experience illness, disease, and conditions within the physical body that have originated from our previous experiences, which are always determined by our thoughts. We may carry these thoughts from lifetime to lifetime until we choose to heal them. In this way, a current condition that we are experiencing may be karmic in nature.

Illness as a Spiritual Awakening

In our culture, illness and disease are often viewed as conditions that must be attacked and destroyed. This is particularly true given the invasive nature of many allopathic treatments and remedies in use today. Cancer cells (as well as healthy cells) are killed through radiation and chemotherapy. Bacteria are attacked by administering antibiotics that have been over prescribed. Stress neuroses are numbed by giving prescriptions of dangerous tranquilizers that may cause dependency and depression is primarily treated by synthetic drugs with many side effects. Up until recently, the deeper connection of the mind and body has been largely ignored by the bulk of modern medical practitioners. Thankfully, this is changing as more medical schools and hospitals are no longer viewing illness as solely a physical phenomenon and have started to address the psychological and spiritual components of illness. Healthcare practitioners and the public are opening to a more expanded awareness that there is indeed a connection between our bodies and our emotions.

As a metaphysical healer and counselor, I have become keenly aware of the purpose that illness and disease serve in our lives. I have observed how one's emotions, if left unbalanced, can and do create stress and imbalance in the physical body. Most importantly, I have seen how illness can serve as a spiritual awakening for the individual suffering from it. All illness serves a purpose in this respect, often enabling us to get in touch with areas of our lives that have long needed our attention. Paradoxically, we create the experience of illness to heal ourselves.

Please note: No one consciously creates or plans to be sick! This is a misconception of many "New Age" proponents who have mistakenly led themselves and others to believe that a person is directly to blame for having a disease. The last emotion an individual needs to be carrying around when he or she is ill is guilt! Yes, we are responsible for our thoughts and our lives in every respect. Yes, we do, in a sense, create imbalances that make us sick. But no, we need never *blame* ourselves for being in this state. "As terrifying as disease is, it is also an invitation to enter into the nature of mystery," says medical intuitive Carolyn Myss in the introduction to *Why People Don't Heal and How They Can* (Harmony Books, 1997.) We can use our experience of illness to find and explore our "essential sacredness."

The single most powerful aspect of any illness is its power to transform us. This process may happen quickly or slowly, depending on our level of personal and spiritual awareness and the corresponding amount of resistance we have to that awareness. Rarely have I met or heard of an individual who was not changed in some way as the result of experiencing serious illness or disease. Of course, the lesson of illness can be used just like any other in our lives—to our advantage, or detriment. If we can view and use illness and disease as the spiritual "wake-up" calls that they are, we can move away from the identity of being a victim and into the realization of self-empowerment. We can even become examples for others' recovery from the same condition. A personal example illustrates this quite beautifully.

I have had the joy of knowing a woman who is a testament to the transformative power of illness. Judith is an attractive, compassionate and vivacious woman in her mid-forties who was diagnosed with lupus a few years prior to our first meeting. Severely debilitated with seizures and unable to walk, she had undergone many treatments in some of the best hospitals in a nearby city. In addition to the regular standardized regimens routinely prescribed for lupus, Judith also chose to use guided imagery, stress-reduction techniques and music therapy for her condition. Additionally, she maintained a regular meditation practice that enabled her to keep in touch with her spirit. She connected with nature as often as possible, used aromatherapy, and journaled on a regular basis. As a result, Judith is an exemplary case of using a holistic approach to heal from a chronic progressive condition. Symptom free and in remission, she volunteers her time to help others heal from lupus, educates others about the disease, and leads guided imagery sessions in a local hospital. The journey of recovery has connected her more intimately with her sacred purpose and enabled her to help others on the same pathway. Whenever I meet with Judith, I am strongly impressed with the power and radiance of her spirit, especially since I know that she has been through so much in her healing journey. She is a shining example of the transformation that can occur through the experience of healing from illness.

Sometimes we may manifest a condition to learn particular soul qualities that we cannot learn in any other way. When we are sick, we certainly cannot conduct our lives in the usual manner to which we are accustomed. Sometimes, an illness teaches us to incorporate the quality of patience into our lives. This is particularly true of chronic conditions that require long-term attention and care. Determination, fortitude and self-nurturing are also qualities that can be learned through illness. Caring for a condition in our physical body forces us to pay mind to taking care of ourselves in the most fundamental ways. As mentioned before, the physical body is the most basic level at which we can meet and balance karma. Our unhealed issues become difficult to ignore when we are in pain, which commands our immediate attention. Illness and disease can be used as a bridge to self-understanding, serving a significant purpose in our spiritual growth.

The two most prevalent diseases in the United States today are heart disease and cancer. Although billions of dollars have been spent on research and cures, many people continue to be afflicted with these conditions. Fortunately more emphasis is being placed on the preventability of these conditions, as health practitioners become aware of the mind-body connection and its significance in the manifestation of disease. The incorporation of complementary medicine departments in some hospitals is evidence of the medical field's growing awareness of the relative importance of non-traditional healing modalities in treating disease. Many of these complementary programs include meditation for stress reduction, acupuncture, massage and energetic healing modalities, such as Reiki. Herbal and homeopathic treatments are likewise being investigated and sought as effective and valuable methods of treatments. This is mostly due to the fact that they tend to carry little or no side effects, and work *with*, not against, the body's natural harmonic balance.

Still largely ignored, however, is the vital connection between the *spirit* and the body. Until this important link is recognized and accepted, we will continue to treat only the surface causes of illness, which do not take into account its spiritual basis, and transformative value in one's life.

Millions of individuals' lives have been significantly and permanently changed due to the experience of illness and disease. Whether it is cancer, heart disease, an immune system disorder or some other life-threatening condition, the healing journey undertaken is fundamentally the same. A person must face the challenges of living life from a different perspective than before the illness. Sometimes this means simply slowing down the pace of one's life to examine facets of life that would not have been looked at if illness had not occurred. Other times, illness functions in our lives to allow us to understand our priorities. Most of us have met a person who, as a result of illness, came to realize what really mattered in life. Some people experience dramatic transformation and completely alter their lives as a result. An example of this is the person who changes careers because of the relative stress levels in one career compared to the other. Another instance of this is the individual who undergoes a striking personality change, becoming more patient, compassionate or loving.

Another significant consideration in the spiritual lessons of illness is the effect it has on the family and friends of the individual. Because the family is a system and each member is affected by another, it is often the case that the illness of one can transform the lives of the others. This is true whether the individual is a child or an aging adult. On a soul level, we make agreements with our families, friends and significant others to both teach and learn lessons that are in accordance with our soul's purpose at the time. We are often not consciously aware of these contracts, although they certainly do exist. On the earth plane, there are many different vehicles the soul can use to advance its purpose spiritually. That is the reason why the soul chooses to express in the physical world of form in the first place. Illness serves as one of these vehicles, affording us the opportunity to shed limitations in the wake of pain and hardship. Because of its innate perfection as the core essence of the Divine, the soul does not experience, perceive or interpret any earthly hardship as devastating or insurmountable, but rather as a pathway enabling further growth and enlightenment on its journey. It is our limited view of the role of illness and disease that causes us to view them primarily as suffering, and not opportunities for growth. For example, an individual in a family may have to sustain caregiving for another with a serious or life-threatening illness. By doing so, she may come to understand and develop spiritually unlike any other situation that she would ordinarily encounter. A client, Nancy, serves as an example of this.

Nancy was having major disagreements with her two sisters over the care of their mother, who required attention because of a heart condition. Her sisters wanted Nancy to do more, despite the fact that she worked full time as a nurse and was a single parent of two children. The pressures of the responsibilities that Nancy faced made her feel extremely frustrated and guilty. In our session, it became clear that her sisters were really the ones who needed to care for their mother, because they were choosing to learn the lessons of patience, nurturing and tolerance that their mother's condition presented. Nancy's lesson in this circumstance was to release the guilt and emotional burden that she had carried for years as a result of her feelings of responsibility for the welfare of others. Since childhood, Nancy had assumed the archetypal roles of both the Savior (one who takes on everyone's problems and tries to "fix" them) and the Scapegoat (one who accepts and shoulders others' blame, guilt and responsibilities.) These are common identities that many people assume to meet karmic circumstances or emotionally survive within the family unit. Over time, these roles become extremely limiting and increasingly dysfunctional in the expression of self. Today, Nancy is aware of how she has allowed herself to become defined by these roles and is making strides towards releasing them. After our last meeting, Nancy decided to stand up to her sisters, affirming that she had done her part in the situation. She understood how her mother's illness taught her about healing herself.

This is one example of how we can utilize another's illness as a catalyst for personal growth. The transformation we experience is a direct result of our willingness to examine the particular lessons inherent in the situation presented to us.

I know an older couple, Joe and Betty, who have been married for nearly 55 years. Joe was employed as the vice-president of a large manufacturing firm before his retirement. About eight years ago, Betty was diagnosed with Alzheimer's disease. Although she is still physically ambulatory and mentally coherent, Betty requires Joe's assistance at times to do even the simplest of daily tasks: cooking, cleaning, and getting dressed in the morning. For most of his life, Joe had been a perfectionist, an analytical thinker and the breadwinner of the family. He believed his role was to be the family provider and take care of the "masculine" duties around the house, such as home and car repairs. He had never cooked, cleaned or done any household chores. Since Betty's diagnosis, however, Joe has undergone remarkable changes by helping to run the household and becoming generally more nurturing. It is amazing to see how much Joe has been able to adapt to caring for Betty. He cooks, cleans and does the chores that Betty used to do. He nurtures Betty by giving her massages, helping her to dress, and administering her medication. Because of Betty's illness, Joe has changed his beliefs about his ability to nurture another. As a result, he has embraced more of his spiritual identity. The transformation in Joe has been quite dramatic, considering his former aversion to the caretaking that is now a major part of his life.

In the face of challenging situations in our lives, we need to ask our inner guidance what we are to learn from the situation. Sometimes we may not readily receive the answer to that inquiry and we must simply go forward in faith, trusting our inner voice. We may not know why we are the one chosen to take care of a sick parent, why we were diagnosed with breast cancer, or why, despite the best medical efforts, our child is still suffering from an incurable disease. Yet if we allow ourselves to trust in the perfect nature of the soul and the element of divine timing, we can move from a position of feeling victimized to one of empowerment. Faith is not the magical wand that cures everything instantaneously, but rather the quiet understanding of the patient mind that rests in the "unknowing."

Emotional Healing

Because our emotions are intricately connected with our physical health, they must necessarily be addressed and healed along with the physical body. In fact, most physical illnesses have a very strong link to the emotional body and often show up there before manifesting in the physical body. If we block awareness of our emotions and what they are communicating to us, chances are we will have to pay the consequences in our body. An example of this is heart disease, which often corresponds with an individual's level of stress from holding toxic emotions such as anger, fear, self-centeredness, bitterness and resentment.

Often a person undergoes an entire change of personality as a result of experiencing a heart attack. He becomes more aware of how he is relating to life and how he has literally hardened the heart to experiencing unconditional love in his life. He may become more willing to examine his priorities in life, such as relationships and family versus a stressful, demanding career. With this re-evaluation of life, he learns to express those aspects of himself that have long remained blocked. This does not necessarily indicate that the physical condition will disappear, but rather that the emotional imbalance will no longer need to be expressed physically.

It is vital that we become aware of and express our emotions. Many people do not grasp the enormous consequences of holding onto toxic emotions for any length of time. If left unchecked, the toxicity of anger, resentment and fear affects us at a cellular level like poison. In order to completely heal an illness, we must face and heal our emotions. In the process, we also positively affect our families, friends and communities by clearing and releasing emotional blocks that prevent us from experiencing love in our lives. When we heal, the world heals—it is no less dramatic than that. One person can impact millions, as history has proven many times.

Stages of Healing the Emotions

As with any process, there are stages to healing that must be recognized and understood in order to move through them with a greater ease. The first is *awareness*. We must recognize that an emotional imbalance does indeed exist. The pain, grief, chaos, anger or emptiness that we feel are messengers from our soul's depths, telling us to awaken to the fact that we have lost touch with our core essence of love. This stage may seem obvious, but in reality, many people walk around for years feeling miserable without a clue that they can feel anything but miserable. In order to heal, we have to be cognizant of the fact that there is an imbalance. Sometimes this awareness comes through the intervention of our angels and spirit guides. They may direct us to a place, person or thing that will enable us to open our eyes to a situation. Other times, the awareness may come through family and friends acting as our teachers by mirroring our unhealed issues. We may see our situation clearly reflected in the actions, attitudes and behaviors of others. Whatever the circumstance, the point is that we become aware of the need to heal.

We then need to become *willing* to heal what is out of balance. Without willingness, we cannot move forward on the pathway. Because all healing comes from within, we must be the one who makes the decision to initiate it. No one can do it for us. I have seen people take the first step to recognize issues that need to be healed, but fail to develop the willingness to follow through. The best way to do this is to pray and ask for the willingness to proceed. Our free will must be brought into accordance with divine will. When we ask for the willingness to heal past wounds, we are really asking that our heart be healed from fear, anger and resentment. Without willingness, we remain stuck in the stage of merely knowing what needs to be healed, and cannot transition into the next stage of *seeking* our healing.

In the third stage, we become actively involved in our healing process: we *seek*, find and follow a healing pathway that is most appropriate for us. For some individuals, this may be traditional psychotherapy. For others, healing the emotional ties that bind may encompass the use of spiritual and energetic techniques such as hypnosis, past life regression, hands-on healing modalities, Ro-Hun therapy (a fast acting energy-based psychotherapy) and others. All pathways to healing are valid and the value of any lies in the individual's response to a particular method. In my experience, energy-based release therapies work much more rapidly than those that are not energy-based. This is because energy healing often bypasses the conscious mind and goes to the root of the imbalance, which is in the subconscious mind. The techniques that work directly with the chakra system also seem to work more rapidly and are able to reach core thoughts that may be blocking an individual. A combination of modalities may be beneficial as well.

An important aspect of the third stage is commitment. We have a much better chance of healing if we are committed to the process. No matter what else is going on in our lives, we must remain dedicated to the healing process. With commitment, the continuity of the healing process stays intact. This enables us to become and remain connected to crucial breakthroughs in our consciousness that occur during the process. Additionally, staying committed allows us to reach deeper levels of awareness that may not occur if we permit distractions to lead us away from the healing process.

Another facet of this stage is transition. Any time that we decide to make changes in our life, we move from one space of consciousness to another. In the book *Extension of Life* by Patricia Hayes and Marshall Smith, (Dimensional Brotherhood Publishing, 1986), the stages of transition are explained by using the analogy of crossing a bridge. Before one makes the decision to move into a new space, he is standing on one side of the bridge. The moment he decides to change his thoughts about where he wants to be, he begins to move across the bridge. There are distinct signs along the way that he is moving into a new space: confusion, fear, disillusionment, disorientation, loss of former familiar thinking patterns, and sometimes depression. When change begins to occur, nothing feels as it did before. Life may become chaotic until he is settled into his new space on the other side of the bridge. Although he can still retain sight of his old familiar space, he has already made the decision to move into his new one. There is no going back and he has a strong desire for his life to be settled once again. When he reaches the other side of the bridge, he is now in his new space.

The feelings that we experience during the transition phase may be intense, overwhelming and unsettling. It may feel as if the very core of our identity is being challenged. We may feel restless, emotionally subdued or angry. We may also go through the process of evaluating our life choices and priorities. Often, we will base any decisions we must now make on the evaluation of where we have been. During this phase it is crucial that we remain committed to the process and continue the journey. We can rest assured that peace and order will again be restored. In fact, we can use our intent to put forth the thought that balance, gentleness and unconditional love surround our healing process.

The fourth and final stage of healing the emotions is *integration*. We are now able to fully assimilate the shifts in our consciousness that have resulted from the particular healing pathway we have sought. Firmly standing in our new space, we begin to act in accordance with our new identity. Although we may retain thoughts and memories of the place we left behind, we have made the necessary changes to successfully release it. Life becomes more settled and once again feels secure. We have adapted to our new way of life and feel a renewed sense of purpose.

The following example is a good illustration of the process involved in healing emotions It concerns the healing process one woman has gone through during her divorce.

Wendy is a respected businesswoman in her late 40's. She

holds two jobs: financial administrator of a bank and freelance writer. When she initially came to me for intuitive guidance, Wendy was experiencing problems within her 10-year marriage to Greg, a construction worker who was on disability due to back injuries. The first session we had together focused on Wendy's dissatisfaction with the marriage and what it was teaching her on emotional and spiritual levels. She was *aware* that something needed to change in the relationship, but wasn't certain about what this was. Over the next two years, Wendy came for sessions on a monthly basis. During this time, she continued to experience emotional pain from the dissatisfaction of the relationship, which had deteriorated into a co-dependent one in which Wendy played the roles of Greg's Caretaker and Rescuer (See glossary of energetic archetypes.) She felt as if the entire responsibility of the relationship was on her shoulders. She found herself feeling responsible for Greg's emotional states and began to "mother" him. As one session revealed, Wendy and Greg had shared a prior life in which Wendy was indeed his mother. This left a strong emotional imprint that accounted for the karmic lessons between them. At the same time she felt responsibility for Greg's life, Wendy felt a tremendous resentment for having to carry the entire burden of emotional and financial responsibility in the relationship. Most of her life, she allowed her Perfectionist to dictate what she could and couldn't do. Nothing she did ever seemed good enough for Wendy.

As time went on, Wendy realized that Greg was not going to change and that her happiness was directly dependent upon her *willingness* to change herself. Wendy made the decision to separate from Greg and *seek* healing for the emotional turmoil in her life. She continued regular counseling sessions, hands-on healing sessions, and other energetic release therapies.

Once divorced, she began the forgiveness process that has been so central to her healing. She and Greg are currently on amicable terms although she is still slowly releasing the sadness, pain and disappointment of the relationship. Wendy now understands that she is not responsible for Greg's happiness or lack thereof. She has also had to confront and heal the archetypes of the Rescuer and the Perfectionist, which controlled her behavior and defined her existence. Wendy is nearing resolution of the divorce and has found love again with a man who shares similar interests and life goals. Because she healed many emotional issues, this current partnership is a healthy, balanced one. Wendy continues to *integrate* all of her new thoughts about who she really is without the limiting patterns she once held. She is embracing the authenticity of her spirit and is more fully in a space of self-empowerment.

When we begin to heal our emotions it is important to keep in mind that healing occurs not only in stages, but also in layers. Each thought that we hold has many other thoughts centered around its core. The adjustment within our mental and emotional patterning occurs in the successive release of each layer of these thoughts. Often when we release a thought pattern, another comes to the surface that must also be addressed and healed. To use the analogy of a plant, the core thought is the bulb or root; the adjacent thoughts are the tendrils of the root, which spread into the earth, yet remain attached to the root. In order to heal, we must examine our core thoughts and beliefs about ourselves and how we have allowed them to define our identity.

Our emotions are an expression of the particular thoughts and beliefs we hold. Getting in touch with and healing our emotions is the gateway to healing our body, mind, and spirit. It is vitally important that we recognize *all* of our emotions, without judgment. When they are troubled, I advise people to allow themselves to feel whatever emotion they are currently struggling with. It is far better to recognize and validate an emotion than to suppress it. At times, this calls for rigorous honesty in admitting to ourselves or others exactly how we feel. This is a small price to pay to maintain our health. We must also remove as much emotional "clutter" and stress as possible from our lives. To do this, we need to evaluate our lives to see what works for us, and what doesn't. Many times, we become stuck in patterns and routines that sustain toxic levels of stress. Unless we make changes, we eventually wind up feeling tired most of the time—an indication that we are off balance and subject to illness.

The joy of health is the most precious resource that we possess. To keep it, we must honor our emotions as much as our bodies. Both are the temples of our spirit.

Questions and Exercises for Self-Enlightenment

1. In your journal, list areas of your life that you feel need to be examined and possibly healed. Beside each one, write your feelings about these areas or issues. Be totally honest in your writing.

2. Next, write small steps you can take now to change the circumstances you have listed. Write as many as you can think of and don't worry about when or how you can make the changes. Envision what your life will be like if you make the changes.

3. In the next week, follow through on at least one of the steps you have listed. Make the phone call, send the letter, sign up for the class. Upon doing so, affirm to yourself that you are one step closer to the life you want to have. Congratulate yourself on your willingness to go after what you want.

4. Nurture yourself in every possible way when you are going through the process of change. Be assured that healing *is* occurring in your life and the change feels good. Seek a friend or support group during your transition.

5. Allow yourself time to adjust to your new emotional space. Do not permit fear to keep you from moving forward.

5

THE POWER OF THOUGHT: HOW TO AFFIRM THROUGH DESIRE AND INTENT

In a class I took on the dynamics of spiritual healing, the teacher was trying to impress upon the class the strength and power of our thoughts. He described thoughts as actual living things, with feet that walk to go out and gather other similar thoughts and bring them back to our minds. I have never forgotten this anecdote over the years I've been teaching intuitive development classes and doing hundreds of psychic-intuitive sessions and spiritual healings with people. I have witnessed the reality of the power of thoughts in not only my own life, but in many others' as well.

Although it has become a "New Age" cliché, our thoughts do create our reality—including our physical and emotional health, how much money we make, and our quality of life. If we change our thoughts, we necessarily change our lives. In fact, we are far more powerful than we have even dared to dream. Our thoughts are so powerful that they are the single most deciding factor in our spiritual growth and well-being. Each of us holds the power to manifest what we want and become the very best we can be. The seat of that power resides within our thoughts. What gives rise to our thoughts and causes them to manifest in a material way in our lives?

Desire

Desire is our soul's "fire." It fuels our creative thoughts into tangible results. The combination of desire and purposeful intent propels our thoughts to take form on the physical plane at an accelerated rate. If we want to experience certain conditions in physical reality, we must infuse our will with our emotions to make it happen. The stronger the desire, the more quickly the physical manifestation of our thoughts will occur.

We constantly create situations in our lives through the combination of desire and intent. If we wish to give birth to a particular situation or creative endeavor, we first conceive the thought of doing so. If the project is something we deeply care about or want, we infuse our thoughts with the desire to bring it into reality. As we continue to think about the possibilities and viable options for manifesting it, we gather more thoughts of similar vibration around the "seed" thought. Much like the process of human conception and pregnancy, we allow our creation to mature within our thought body until we are ready to deliver it into physical reality. The entry of desire into our thought process is like the nourishment that a developing fetus obtains from its mother. It is the life-force that our thoughts need to manifest into tangible form.

Vonnie is a good example of a person who has experienced the power of desire operating in her life. In her early forties, Vonnie operated a small newsstand for five years before losing the business to a devastating fire. Unemployed and emotionally depleted, Vonnie felt directionless for nearly a year. During that time, she took a few classes on energy healing because she had developed an interest in it from books she had read. Soon Vonnie started to notice an affinity for helping and healing others. She continued to take classes, enrolled in an advanced healing course and became certified as a spiritual healer. Within the course of a year, Vonnie set up her own full-time healing and counseling practice.

The last time I saw Vonnie, she was glowing with a sense of accomplishment from being of service to others. "I love what I do now and I would never want to change that," she said. "Who would have thought a year ago that I would be doing this and feel so deeply rewarded for it!"

Not all stories of manifesting one's desires are as positive as Vonnie's. Some people I have met have shared stories of their unintentional manifestation of what might be considered negative conditions: illness, accidents, financial bankruptcy or emotional separation from loved ones. Usually, people want to know why such dire circumstances would happen to them. I explain to them that universal life-force energy is impartial; it responds according to the intent behind it. Remember desire is our will fueled by strong emotion. The quality of the emotion does not matter as much as the intensity of it. Nor does the conscious recognition of the emotion count as much as its presence in our thoughts. One can hold emotions such as anger, greed, or resentment at a subconscious threshold for long periods of time. Some people do this for years and eventually manifest cancer or heart disease. If a person is in denial of these lower vibratory emotions, he could actually bring undesirable conditions into physical reality.

Lisa strongly desired to get a different car because the one she owned needed extensive repairs and wasn't fuel-efficient. Every time she drove somewhere, she thought about how much the car drained her financially. She strongly desired to get rid of the car and drive a different one. On her way to work one morning, Lisa was involved in an accident that sent her to the hospital with a concussion and a broken leg. Because her car was nearly totaled, the insurance company reimbursed her for its value, which was only $1500. After she recuperated, the only car Lisa could afford to buy was a second-hand one that was in worse shape mechanically than her old one. Although it didn't use as much gas, the second-hand car was definitely not what she had in mind when she thought about getting rid of the old one. She had gotten what she asked for—she got rid of her old car and got a different one. The universe clearly responded to her thoughts. What Lisa was not expecting was the direction her thoughts took by attracting an "accident" to manifest the much desired different car.

In order to keep our thoughts clear and of a relatively high vibration, it is essential that we do regular "maintenance checks" on the condition of our thinking. I recommend that people clear as much mental debris from their thoughts as possible. Mental debris is any thought that diminishes our innate sense of emotional balance and peace. Stress is a good example of this. Thoughts of love, healing, peace, good will and harmony lift our vibration and resonate with our divine nature. The less entangled our thoughts become with mental debris, the more easily we can use them to manifest situations of love, empowerment, and abundance.

It is amazing how quickly we can realize our desires when we infuse our thoughts with love and commitment that support our sacred purpose in life. Let's look more deeply at how to do this by considering the role that intent plays in the manifestation process.

Intent

Intent is our purpose in performing a specific task or action and is the "compass" that directs our thoughts. Universal life-force energy is neutral until it is backed with the energy of intent. For example, we can use our thoughts to heal (such as prayer) or to harm someone (such as directing thoughts of hate.) The difference lies in the intent behind our thoughts.

Prayer serves as an excellent example of focusing intent. As I became more spiritually aware, I began to evaluate the way I prayed. I began to realize the importance of aligning my will with divine will, instead of asking for a specific desired outcome for the person or situation. I'm much less result-oriented in my prayers and more willing to surrender to the highest pathway for the person or situation even if it's not what I would ultimately want—for example, the death of a loved one. Sometimes, healing through passing into the world of spirit can be exactly what a person needs for spiritual growth. I've come to understand that not all people heal in a specific pattern or according to a timetable. I decided to change the way I thought about prayer and discovered the following to be helpful:

When praying for someone who may be in poor health or undergoing hardship, it is helpful to visualize that person in optimal health and in good spirits. Because thoughts are energy and very real, they will automatically be attracted to the auric or energetic field of the person who is prayed for and lift their vitality. (It is not necessary to know the person; a name will suffice since it draws in the specific vibration of that person.) This is why prayer has such a healing effect, which has been well documented by many recent studies. Although the exact mechanics may not be completely understood, I believe it helps the healing process because it sets up a magnetic resonance in which the vibrations of health, wholeness and vitality reach critical mass in the field of the recipient. Once that occurs, the energy field may more quickly return to a state of equilibrium and health.

At times, the best remedy we can offer to a friend or loved one in distress is prayer. The healing energy of a simple prayer should not be underestimated in its ability to make a difference in any situation. When I connect with loved ones who have recently passed into the spirit world, I advise the client to pray for their continued spiritual growth and happiness. If a person was troubled emotionally before passing, prayer helps to uplift and heal the individual after crossing over. It also makes the transition and adjustment from the physical plane to the spirit world smoother for a passing spirit.

Is it possible to use one's intent to deliberately harm another? Black magic—or manipulative use of life-force energy to harm another—is an ancient practice that still exists today. Intent to gain control over another is usually the motivating factor behind most black magic. (Again, it is the force of the intent behind the thoughts that determine the effect of the energy sent.) "Psychic attack", directing thoughts of anger, hatred, lust or jealousy toward a person, either intentionally or unintentionally, is a reality. Many people are unaware that such forces are real and can be harmful if one is open to them. To be vulnerable to such forces one must, on some level, be open to receiving these negative thoughts from another. This is often the result of poor self-esteem, unclear and poorly defined boundaries, and/or an auric field that is weakened through the use of alcohol or drugs. To protect yourself from harmful thoughts, shield your aura in white light surrounded by a layer of violet light at all times, especially before sleeping.

We are the Sum Total of Our Thoughts

Intent and desire fuel most of our thoughts and are the essential energies that ignite all physical manifestation. Every action is preceded by a thought and everything in the physical world was first a thought. That is why we truly do create our own reality every minute of every day. Each person, event, circumstance and thing in our lives is a result of some thought we hold or held at some time. Even our physical bodies are the accumulation of our thoughts from both this and previous lifetimes. Depending on the state of our consciousness, we enjoy either health (which is proper alignment of life-force energetic flow) or illness (which is the result of imbalance within our energetic flow.)

The vibration of our thoughts is the single most determining factor in the overall quality of the life we create and express daily. Fear-based emotions such as anger, fear, selfishness and envy are of a lower vibration than those of harmony, love, generosity and compassion. The more frequently we are able to fill our minds and hearts with positive, loving thoughts and feelings, the better our lives become in terms of health, well-being and prosperity. Most, if not all, discord in the world today—including war, murder, and racial injustice—is a result of people holding thoughts that are fear-based. To heal the world and ourselves we must transcend hatred and fear, and lift our thoughts into healing vibrations of love, compassion, peace and forgiveness. If we do not, we will continue to experience painful reminders that we are out of touch with our true nature, which is love.

Each day we need to cleanse and instill our minds with peaceful, loving thoughts. A good time to do this is in the morning when we are preparing to start another day. I have found that when I give thanks for another day and for all the blessings in my life, I set a loving tone for the day. This sets up the resonance for other positive thoughts to be drawn to me like a magnet and I find my day going smoothly. Here are other helpful mind "tools" that can be used to clear and work with your thoughts.

Visualization

Visualization is the technique of using specific imagery within our minds for a desired outcome. This process is especially helpful and highly effective in not only manifesting a specific outcome, but also in altering ingrained emotional patterns and beliefs. Because the subconscious mind operates much like a tape recorder that is continually on, it contains all of our experiences, both past and present. (Some metaphysicians believe that it contains our future experiences, as well.) Just like the magnetic recording tapes we use in tape players and video units, the fabric of the subconscious is imprinted with impressions that are being recorded onto it by the vibration of our thoughts. Until we erase the imprint, it remains present in our consciousness, affecting us in ways that are sometimes baffling and destructive to our well-being.

Through the process of visualization, we can imprint new images of ourselves—including what we want to bring into our lives, what we wish to release and even how we want to look. Imagine that you desire to lose 20 pounds and wish to use the process of visualization to improve your results. Visualize yourself being 20 pounds lighter. Perhaps you have a photograph of yourself at your ideal weight; you could look at this picture daily and image it on your internal viewing screen, or mind's eye. You can even picture a huge movie screen and project your chosen image upon it. Repeat this process at least several times during the day and particularly at night before drifting off to sleep. Why? Each time you imprint the image of yourself being at your ideal weight, you are sending a powerful message to your subconscious mind, which happens to be most actively engaged during your sleeping hours.

Two important considerations to keep in mind when doing the process: be very specific about the desired results, and repeat the exercise often. The more specific we can be in what we want, the better our chance of manifesting it. This means that we must *focus* while doing visualizations. In the weight loss example, the photo helps us to focus on the desired outcome. In other situations, we may have to engage our imagination to concentrate on a potential outcome. This is fine because the realm of imagination in the right brain contains much creative energy, which can be used to enhance the manifestation process.

Affirmations and the Subconscious Mind

Affirmations are another tool that can be used to positively work with our thoughts. Affirmations are positive statements that are usually pronounced with the words "I am" in the beginning, followed by the quality, situation or action we wish to claim or manifest. For example, "I am radiantly healthy," "I am loving," or "I am opening myself to healing energy now."

Affirmations are always said in the present tense because we want to claim that quality or state of being with the power of the present moment. Repeated silently or aloud, affirmations are vehicles for personal growth and transformation. They help to restructure and reinforce belief patterns. Have you ever heard the old adage that if you are told something enough, you begin to believe it? This is particularly true in our impressionable childhood years. It is also true when we are adults.

To understand how affirmations work, it is necessary to realize the mechanics of the subconscious mind. As stated before, the subconscious mind records all of our life experiences—good and bad. There is no filtering mechanism in this part of our consciousness. The analogy of the tape recorder is a good one to understand the mechanism of the subconscious. If we carried the recorder with us for a single day and left it on at all times (assuming we had long tapes!) it would record all of our unedited conversations, background noise and any audible sounds in our environment. There would be no filtering of any sort.

The subconscious mind stores all of our past life memories in vivid detail as well as all childhood memories and experiences including our prenatal time, birth and early bonding memories. Every event, conversation and emotional/ psychological experience we have ever had is stored within the domain of the subconscious. Carl Jung, the first psychologist to document research on the collective unconscious (also called universal mind or universal consciousness) believed that an individual's subconscious mind is a subset of the collective unconscious and that archetypal (original models) memories and patterns could be found there. Among many other things, Jung is credited with studying the interconnectedness of the human mind with cosmic or higher consciousness.

Because there is no filter in the subconscious, it will readily accept whatever information is put into it. The bits of information imprinted upon it, like recording tape, are stored automatically. Much, if not all, of our waking existence is controlled by the subconscious. Although we are not aware of it, we often act and react from patterns of belief imprinted on our subconscious minds. Our conscious mind will filter and analyze experiences, but it cannot stop the process of recording onto our subconscious. The conscious mind constantly seeks order and structure and is the domain of logic, analysis and rational thought. Through the use of affirmations, we can address our recorded belief patterns, sometimes from many lifetimes ago. The power of these positively spoken words can effectively transform and restructure limiting beliefs that have been detrimental to our psychological health and well-being.

Following is a list of healing affirmations that can be used daily. Remember to say them several times a day and especially before going to sleep at night. It is often helpful to write them either in a journal or on paper that can be displayed prominently in a place you will frequently see them, such as a bathroom mirror.

I AM . . .

. . . richly abundant in all facets of my life.

. . . radiantly and fully healthy.

. . . opening myself each moment to the abundance of the universe.

. . . loving, loved and lovable.

. . . worthy to receive all the good things life has to offer me.

. . . attracting to me all that is for my highest and best good now.

. . . forgiving the past and releasing the wounds of yesterday.

. . . living my life in harmony, balance and love.

. . . trusting my intuition to guide me in the pathway of my purpose.

. . . a divine child of God who deserves the very best life has to offer.

You may write your own affirmations to energize and heal any area of your life. Simply begin the statement with the words "I am" followed by the quality you wish to attract. Because we already contain the divine blueprint for every quality in the universe, it is possible for us to attract and energize any quality we wish by adjusting our beliefs and thoughts to match it. We must embrace the quality we desire to experience by acting as if we already possess it. In doing this, it is possible to rewrite our life script and open to a greater level of reception to the full abundance of the universe.

Questions and Exercises for Self-Enlightenment

1. In your journal, list one quality, event, situation or project that you desire to energize or make real in your life. Now write your intent for making this happen. Your intent should answer the question, "Why do I want to make this happen?" Be specific.

2. Next, list at least three things you can do to make your idea a reality. These do not have to be major steps in the process, but should be realistic in that you can easily do them. For example, if I want to energize the quality of giving in my life, I may list volunteering two hours weekly to a nonprofit organization; assisting a friend or relative with chores and errands, and tithing extra funds to a cause of my choice.

3. Write several affirmations that match the quality or situation you wish to realize. Say, write and post them daily.

4. Visualize yourself actively doing, being and/or having what you want. Energize the picture with your feelings. Make it as real as you can. See and feel all the details.

5. Stay in the moment. Congratulate yourself for being open to expansion and growth. Focus on your desire daily and celebrate even the smallest accomplishments so they will expand.

PART TWO

The Chakras:
Vortices Of Light And Consciousness

Throughout this book you will find numerous references to the chakras, seven energy centers in the body through which we sustain and maintain our spiritual, mental, emotional and physical existence. Because the charkas are so central to understanding ourselves, it is essential to have a basic comprehension of each one and its role in the process of interpreting and creating our experiences.

"Chakra" is a Sanskrit word meaning "spinning wheel." These portals or vortices channel vital energy from universal sources that enters and exits our consciousness and our physical body. Located on the etheric energy body (see glossary), they connect to all levels of our being—mind, body and soul. They are formed when we decide to come to the physical plane and they continue to operate as long as we are here.

All of our thoughts and experiences from every lifetime are stored within our subconscious mind, and they are expressed in our chakra system as well. This is why it is possible to identify the root causes of imbalance and disease within the chakras through intuitive healing techniques that bypass the conscious mind. We are the sum total of our thought patterns, and we distribute our life-force energy according to the nature of these thoughts. Since most of our thinking and behavior is directed by our subconscious mind, it is essential that when we begin the process of healing, we focus on reaching this part of ourselves. There are many techniques for doing this—including hypnosis (addresses and releases subconscious thought patterns for healing); past-life regression (releases unbalanced thoughts and emotions from prior incarnations) and spiritual healing (transmits divine energy by a gentle laying-on of hands.) Each of these healing modalities may be used alone or in combination, depending on the needs of the client.

There is a host of detailed studies written on the chakra system. One of the most comprehensive is *The Chakras and the Human Energy Fields* by S. Karagulla, M.D. and Dora Van Gelder Kunz (Theosophical Publishing House, 1989). Van Gelder Kunz, one of the greatest clairvoyants of the century, describes each of the energy centers in detail—including color, size and rate of velocity. Because she was able to see each chakra, there are case studies of her diagnosis of disease through her visual analysis of the centers. These studies lend support to the belief that when there is illness or disease within the body, the chakras will reflect this by varying from their normal color and flow patterns. This can then be verified by medical testing that shows there is illness present.

Another excellent study of the chakras can be found in Caroline Myss' *Anatomy of the Spirit* (Crown Pub. Inc.1996). Myss, a medical intuitive, writes about the seven stages of power and healing that we undertake on the journey through the chakra system. The insights she relates from her case studies and experiences in energy medicine are particularly useful in the interpretation of each center. She discusses the correlation between each chakra and the spiritual consciousness that it reflects. A valuable resource guide to reference when studying the chakras, this book has shed new light on the emerging field of energy medicine and its usefulness in the diagnosis and healing of disease.

When we are functioning at a normal level of health, each one of the chakras is spinning at an optimal rate with very little or no impediment. The quality and vibration of our thoughts, both past and present, are the determining factors in the general state of our health. Karma (the law of cause and effect) that we have brought with us into our present incarnation also affects the chakra system. As discussed in Chap 4, many illnesses, both physical and mental, have their roots in karmic experiences.

In their most basic form, each chakra represents a level of consciousness reflecting our spiritual development towards union with the Divine. Each one resonates to a different quality that we must master on our journey towards self-enlightenment. No one center is more important than another, each being a necessary energy that we incorporate in the process of spiritual growth.

It is key to remember that the centers must be understood as a *system;* that is, each part affects every other one and the whole is one operating unit. If we accept the premise that there is no separation in the universe, that everything is a part of everything else, we can understand that the chakra system is similarly interrelated within itself and to our spiritual, mental, emotional and physical bodies. There is a tenet in metaphysical philosophy which simply stated says "As above, so below." If we apply this to the chakras, when we are experiencing imbalance in one center, we will automatically experience it in some form on another level of consciousness or in another of the seven centers.

From the moment of birth until we take our final breath, we are learning how to distribute our divine life-force energy. Each day, this energy is sent through our chakras, which filter and process the information. On a daily basis, we are given the grand opportunity to "rewire" our circuitry and learn new lessons. Because we have been given the gift of free will, we are eternally able to change our minds and hearts concerning the distribution of this energy. This is why *all* healing is generated from within. Let's explore the particular qualities and functions of each chakra.

(Note: You will find the most commonly accepted interpretations of each chakra's characteristics. I have included the Sanskrit name and its general translation. Some studies may contain varying information about color vibrations, gemstones, and emotional correspondences. I am basing my interpretations on my own observations through doing healing work.)

6

THE LOWER CHAKRAS

Root Chakra—Earth

The root chakra (*muladhara-"root"*) corresponds to the area located at the base of the spine. Energetically this center connects to the legs, feet, large intestine, and is associated with the functioning of the immune system. The root chakra is the center that grounds us and enables us to take physical form. It is connected to spiritual, mental and emotional support of all types—including religion, family, and society. Our ability to feel secure is also in the domain of the root, as is our basic need to belong. Tribal instincts—the deep, often subconscious bonds we share with one another—are found at this level of our consciousness. Whenever we are threatened in any way we react from this core part of ourselves. Striking examples of this have occurred historically when our nation has been at war when many people feel both physically and emotionally vulnerable. During these times, people bond at the most basic levels. For example, during WWII, American citizens showed support for their country by donating blood to the Red Cross, expressing loyalty to overseas troops, and buying war bonds.

These demonstrations of loyalty created a sense of unity and strength among people. As a result, Americans experienced a new resurgence of patriotism and national identity. The atrocities of the war, especially in the Nazi concentration camps, provided a catalyst for people worldwide to examine their collective belief systems regarding respect for human life and dignity.

After the Sept. 2001 terrorist attacks in New York and Washington, D.C., many people didn't feel safe anymore. Again, our root chakra energies were brought to light to examine and heal. Did we take our safety for granted? To this day, security measures in most public buildings remain heightened. Air travel declined because of passengers' inability to feel secure in airports and planes. Most people began to pay attention to their physical safety as never before. In a fundamental way, everyone bonded as human beings— race, nationality and religion did not divide us.

Our family of origin is our tribe when we are born. During infancy and childhood, we bond emotionally with our tribe. Loyalty, ability to provide, and physical sustenance are all found in the consciousness of the root. In childhood, we are (hopefully) nurtured and supported by our family. Unfortunately, many children are not given the necessary emotional nourishment and must seek it outside of the family. An example of this is found in "gangs." Often, many young people join gangs in an effort to belong to a group that makes them feel secure and valued. The same could be said in a more benevolent sense about sports teams and college sororities and fraternities. Group identity provides us with bonding, stability and a sense of belonging. Without the association of the group, we are left feeling emotionally vulnerable and ungrounded.

Our biological, ancestral, national, and cultural tribes affect us at a deep level and we are subject to their beliefs, fears and prejudices. Some people spend a lifetime attempting to overcome and heal unbalanced group belief patterns that they were exposed to as a child. So strong is our bond with our tribal identity that in order to change it, we must use healing modalities that touch us at a core level, such as hypnosis or regression. Yet we must keep in mind that we are a mirror for the tribe and vice versa. The tribe may reflect our shadow or "dark" side, but they are nonetheless us and we are they. On a soul level we have chosen to be born into *all* of our circumstances, and it is up to us to understand what personal lessons our tribe or group consciousness is reflecting to us, then balance those energies within ourselves.

I have counseled people who have spent substantial portions of their lives trying to belong to this group or that. Many have felt the need to relocate numerous times to different geographical locations, never knowing why they felt the need to continually be on the move. Some have tried different spiritual practices to gain a sense of power from the identity of different systems of thought. Until we ground our presence here on the earth to the secure anchor that comes from our own internal sense of being, we are destined to search for external sources that can never really replace our own. I have known women and men who are looking to fill the void of an emotionally distant parent with an equally emotionally distant spouse or partner. One client, Ken, had great difficulty in relationships due to a supercritical mother who never accepted him as he was. He constantly chose partners who reflected his mother's perfectionism and then wondered why he felt so defensive toward them. Because of the pain of these relationships, he began to examine the emotional issues of his childhood in order to release the toxic patterns that had been set up. Since we all choose our particular incarnating circumstances based on our soul's lessons in a lifetime, we can begin to heal the root energies from our childhood by using all of our relationships as teaching opportunities that reflect back to us our unhealed identities.

In addition to being the seat of our physical identity, the root chakra is the natural resting place for the *kundalini*, which is latent life-force energy. In the religious teachings of Buddhism and Hinduism, this fiery force is depicted as a sleeping serpent, coiled around three times, resting at the base of the spine. It begins to awaken naturally and spontaneously when an individual seeks enlightenment through spiritual awareness. The great yogic masters of India dedicate their lives to the arousal and subsequent movement of the kundalini through the chakra system. In a person who is becoming spiritually aware, the kundalini energy will move slowly through the chakras in a natural pathway that unblocks the chakras in the process of healing previously unbalanced resistances. During this time, an individual's unresolved emotional issues will surface for examination and release. These blockages may also show up in a physical illness, such as heart disease, for clearing, release and balance. Because the kundalini is such an incredibly powerful force, its arousal and movement should never be forced, but should happen naturally to prevent overload to the emotions and physical body. One of the best ways to safely raise the kundalini is through the practice of kundalini yoga, which incorporates specific breathing exercises, postures, and mantras.

Red is the color vibration of the root chakra. It resonates to the key of C. Corresponding gemstones are garnet, ruby, hematite and bloodstone. Any substance that is of the earth resonates to the energy of the root. Connecting with the earth through nature, drumming, and daily physical exercise are ways of healing and balancing the root.

Questions and Exercises For Self-Enlightenment

1. What is my relationship with my family of origin? What belief patterns do I share with them? With which ones do I differ? Why?

2. List the tribes in your life. Include as many as you can, including family, friends, political affiliations and clubs to which you belong. What do you have in common with each group? What do you not? How is each group supportive of you?

3. How do I provide for myself on a purely physical level? How safe and secure do I feel in my place of residence? My hometown? My country? If you do not feel safe, you may want to do some visualization exercises in which you see yourself surrounded by pure white light in a protective cocoon. When traveling, call upon your guides and angels for guidance and protection.

4. Connect with the earth as much as possible. Spend time outdoors in natural settings. If it is not possible for you to do so, use meditation and visualization to recall a place you've been that was particularly relaxing. See and feel yourself encompassed and nurtured by the earth. Visit a private garden in your meditation where you are able to use all of your senses to experience the smells, sights, and sounds of the earth. Record in your meditation journal.

5. Buy or make a drum. Drumming is an activity that resonates with the vibration of the earth. Better yet, sit on the floor and drum! By doing so, you will connect your root chakra directly with the earth. It is also fun and healing to do group drumming and bond with others who are looking to form similar connections.

The Spleen Chakra—Emotion and Relationships

Located in the lower abdominal area, a few inches below the navel, is the spleen or sacral center. The Sanskrit word for this chakra is *svadhisthana,* meaning "sweetness." The genitals, hips, lower back, bladder, appendix, and ovaries are located in the energetic domain of this center.

The spleen chakra is the location of our emotional presence. Our primary need to form relationships with others is also the domain of the second center, as is the need to exert some measure of control over our lives and those around us. The Inner Child (the purity, innocence, and creativity of the soul) resides here, as do most of our basic emotional responses. As the location for our creative energies, the spleen center is where we begin to experience the use of power both in relationship to others and ourself.

In the physical body, the hips are the center of balance and gravity. When a child first learns to walk, he must learn to balance the hips and feet exactly to maintain his equilibrium, lest he topple over. He must learn to balance his upper and lower body while motor skills are being developed. It is interesting to note that learning to walk is followed by the "terrible twos," in which the child learns he is not the only human being on earth who has needs, wants and desires. He also learns that he is distinct and separate from his parents and siblings (the tribe).

From the time we are very young, we learn about the use and misuse of power. Most of us grew up in families where we were rewarded for using our power in constructive ways. We were taught about the concept of sharing with others and we have been socialized in public schools where we interacted with peer groups. Upon entering school, we learn to interact with others and control the raw emotional responses that we had as children. Unfortunately, many people are taught to submerge their emotions and creativity at a young age. We are told to stop daydreaming and to pay attention to more important concerns in the "real" world. This is the reason why so many children lose their awareness of the spirit world around the age of seven. Up until that age, they have not fully activated the filtering mechanism of the left or rational brain. In the world of the preschool child, fairies, angels, and loved ones in spirit are very real and there have been many documented cases of children who have reported seeing such beings. Usually, when children enter first grade, they are encouraged and rewarded for using logical thinking much more than right–brain capacities. This is why it is so essential that as we mature to adulthood, we find ways to keep in touch with and reclaim the Inner Child.

The second chakra is also the location of our sexual instincts, which we must learn to control in a healthy, balanced way during the process of socialization. Many people experience repression at this level and have literally made themselves sick because of blocked sexual energy. Diseases of the pelvic region, urinary tract, and uterus all have their origins in stifled sexual and creative energy of the second chakra.

Mary came in for counseling and healing because of pelvic pain and bleeding. She had a sense that there was more going on than what she was aware of because she felt "confused" about her life. She had recently lost her nursing job due to downsizing in a local hospital and had ended an emotionally dissatisfying marriage. During the session, it was very clear to Mary that she needed to not only heal the past relationship with her ex-husband but to find a new creative outlet for her nursing skills. Because of her family expectations, she had worked in traditional healthcare that allowed her little room for her strong beliefs in complementary medicine. She wanted to blend traditional nursing methods with those of a more alternative nature. I suggested that she apply at several alternative healing clinics and work on forgiving herself and her ex-husband. By taking these steps, Mary was able to begin the process of freeing the trapped energy of the second chakra and reclaim the power of her own being. Like many other disorders, Mary's physical symptoms served a purpose in alerting her to the power of forgiveness and listening to the wisdom of her inner voice. In many instances, we ignore our intuition and do what others tell us to do. We put our own divine calling aside to meet society's or our family's expectations. We lose touch with the Inner Child who reminds us of our soul's purity and creativity. The lesson of the second chakra teaches us to balance our power in relationship to others and to make relationship choices that teach us about ourselves.

In the centuries old divination system of the Tarot, one of the major arcana cards is the Lovers. This card traditionally means choice and decision, particularly as it concerns romantic relationships. It also represents the physical duality of God as expressed in male and female form. The energy expressed by the Lovers' card reflects the lessons of the sacral chakra in that we choose to experience relationships to learn about ourselves in ways that could never be accomplished alone. Through those around us, we learn about balancing both our inherent yin (female) and yang (male) energies, which together make up the unity of divine expression within the individual. In the process of spiritual development, we recognize and integrate the full expression of our soul, regardless of our physical sex. Examples of this include a woman who becomes comfortable in asserting herself through a career, and a man who enjoys nurturing children. The relationships we choose either support us in integrating our full expression or keep us locked into our unhealed emotional patterns. What has caused us the most pain in our relationships? Are there patterns to the types of relationships we choose? What are they showing us?

Because relationships are always acting as a mirror to us,

we can effectively use them as invaluable teaching devices for self-growth by accepting responsibility for our own life, and releasing blame of others. To accomplish this, we must set our egos aside and let our defenses rest long enough to look at what these mirrors are reflecting to us. Until we do, we are destined to repeat the karmic lessons that we have brought with us.

The sacral chakra resonates with the color orange and the key of D. The gemstones of coral and carnelian are used to heal and balance it.

Questions and Exercises For Self-Enlightenment

1. What is the quality of the relationships in my life? Do I find them personally fulfilling? In what ways can I improve them?

2. How do the relationships in my life mirror my inner conflicts? List at least three "hot spots" in your relationships that seem to always come up. What do these problem areas show you about yourself? How might you change them?

3. Find a photo from when you were approximately five years of age. Look into the eyes of the child in the photo and connect with him or her on a soul level. Talk to the child, expressing how you feel. Remember that you have never really been separated from the child; you have simply forgotten that he or she has been with you since birth. Keep the photo in a place where you will see it daily.

4. How do I express male and female qualities in my life? If you are female, are you able to assert yourself when necessary, such as setting healthy boundaries for yourself? If you are male, do you consider yourself nurturing? In order to be truly balanced individuals we need to claim all of our qualities and express them equally. How might you begin to embrace more of your "disowned" qualities?

5. Allow yourself to have creative fun. In fact, make it an absolute priority. Painting, singing, dancing, baking, and woodworking are ways that you can sidestep the rational brain for a while. Become more spontaneous. Allow yourself to live at least one day a month in which there are no "rules." Experience a totally unstructured day without constraints of time, duty or obligation. Journal how it feels for you to be free. Do you feel relief? Guilt? Be totally honest with yourself.

Solar Plexus Chakra-Personal Power

The third energy center, *manipura*, meaning "lustrous gem" in Sanskrit, is located in the midsection of the body's trunk. Many of the vital organs are located in the domain of this chakra: the stomach, liver, gallbladder, pancreas, spleen, kidneys and adrenal glands. One of the main functions of the solar plexus is to absorb and distribute vitality throughout the chakra system and the physical body. Life sustaining energy from the sun and the atmosphere, as well as from the food we eat, is absorbed through the assimilation processes of this center. A developing fetus is joined to its mother at the solar plexus, as this is the site for the umbilical cord that funnels nutrients to it. Besides absorbing atmospheric and physical nutrients, the solar plexus is capable of and often does absorb psychic energy from situations and people around us. It may also function as a seat of intuitive faculties and gut-level "knowing."

Issues of our personal power reside here. These include our self-esteem, self-worth, confidence, responsibility to the outside world, and achievement. "Negative" emotions such as fear, anger, and generalized anxiety are often experienced through the solar plexus as well. Often people will experience physical symptoms within the stomach area when there is an emotion generated through the spleen or other chakras. This center is exquisitely sensitive to our surrounding environment and we literally process bits of information through it. Most of this processing is subconscious—as is the case with all of the chakras—and goes on even when we are asleep.

The third energy center is important in determining the sense of our place in relation to the outside world. When we develop healthy self-esteem, we are deeply aware of our own personal power and how to manage it in a balanced way. From birth on, we constantly learn lessons about our innate power and how to manage it wisely. Many people spend a lifetime dealing with issues of power through career, relationships, or even illness. How we choose to deal with the challenge, of course, makes all of the difference in determining the sense of who we are and ultimately, our place in and relationship to the world around us. Do we stand up assertively to be counted or do we tuck our tail and run for cover? Are we able to feel a sense of pride in our accomplishments in life or do we always allow others the honor and glory? If we are female, are we afraid of our power, concerned that it may make us unattractive? Are we doing work that we love and getting paid a fair salary for it?

I once counseled a woman, Rachel, who was afraid of her own power. She was educated at a prestigious college and held a master's degree in business. She had risen to the ranks of upper-level management in her company and genuinely liked her work. Despite all of this, Rachel had a terrible time managing the people who worked for her. She found herself falling into one of three roles: she mothered them, befriended them, or completely distanced herself from them. Sometimes she thought of them as rivals, people she had to compete against, instead of cooperate with. She also had an issue with losing weight, despite numerous diets and careful eating habits. During two different regression sessions, Rachel went to lifetimes in which she had struggled with asserting her personal power. In an ancient one, she was a female warrior on the battlefield in a matriarchal society who was in charge of leading a group into war to defend the homeland. She reported feeling alone and unsupported by her soldiers, none of whom seemed to care if she lived or died. And die she did, alone on the battlefield, as a relatively young woman. In the second session, she regressed to a lifetime in which she was an intelligent young woman who had been displaced from her family land and subsequently married a well-to-do man primarily because it was expected of her by society at the time. She had led a comfortable life, but one devoid of any pursuit of creative expression, especially her intelligence. Through integration of these two sessions, she was able to make the connection between previous challenges with asserting her personal power and her current life. She discovered that her extra weight served as a form of protection; when she was a warrior, she needed it for survival and strength. As a result of the sessions, Rachel was able to understand and begin the process of healing thought patterns she had held from former experiences.

Nowhere is the issue of personal power highlighted so vividly as in our choice of career and the environment of our workplace. Indeed, many people base their very self-worth and personal identity on their ability to perform in a career setting. Traditionally, this has been much more the case with men, but that is changing as women are assuming more "high profile" positions. As with any area of our lives, we must learn to balance our innate drive for recognition and accomplishment with a sense of unconditional self-acceptance. Too many people desire success at any price and all too often this has taken a serious toll on relationships, family, and health. The popular image of the antacid-eating businessman is one that has become very familiar in our culture of high-stress, performance-oriented workplaces. Many people internalize the stress that inevitably accompanies this drive to succeed. The third chakra is one in which the effects of stress are commonly felt. I have noticed that individuals who are perfectionists and very performance-oriented often have an imbalance within this center. Sometimes it manifests in the physical body in disorders such as indigestion or ulcers; other times the chakra is energetically misaligned, which causes predisposition to illness and stress. Unless the imbalance is healed, illness or disease is likely.

The third chakra teaches us lessons of self-acceptance. If we can learn to give ourselves unconditional approval regardless of the demands put upon us by the outside world, we can become the masters of our destinies. We must also learn to shift the focus of our sense of control from an external source to an internal one. From this standpoint, we become unshakable in our resolve to commit to ourselves. When we are able to focus our energy on maintaining and meeting our own standards of approval, we eliminate falling into the trap of seeking validation from others. Unfortunately, most people are taught from the time they are very young to be competitive, comparative and status-oriented. Although times are changing, our society still places little value on developing the inner senses of intuitive guidance that emanate from the voice of the soul. This is the gut-level knowing that the pathway we choose is the right one for us, no matter what anyone else thinks of our choice. Some of the most painful and transformative events of our lives have to do with reclaiming our innate power that we have given all too freely to situations and others around us. Drained of our vital energy, we retreat from thinking and acting for ourselves, much to the detriment of our self-esteem. Then we wonder why our lives seem meaningless and unfulfilling. Through healing the third chakra, we can welcome the return of the Authentic Self, that part of ourselves that is truly reflective of our divine nature. It is the seed of our very being and cannot be destroyed by anything or anyone.

The ability to set and maintain healthy emotional boundaries is another lesson contained in the solar plexus chakra. This is an extremely common problem for many clients, especially women, who've come to see me. These individuals feel guilty when they say "no," regardless of the situation. Often, they suffer from playing the role of the Martyr, who tries to be everything to everybody in an attempt to compensate for low self-esteem. To heal this imbalance, it is necessary to learn how to claim one's own power and disconnect from others in a healthy way.

Finally, the third center teaches us about the ramifications of personal responsibility. We move from a position of viewing ourselves as the victim, to one of acknowledging our responsibility in creating our own life. With the realization of personal responsibility for everything in our lives, we can come to terms more easily with situations that may seem totally out of our control. The shift in our perception makes all the difference in handling even the most difficult of circumstances. The following example illustrates this quite beautifully.

Diane came for a series of intuitive sessions in which she sought guidance about her inability to break free from her controlling mother's influence. Even though she was in her mid-30's, Diane was still very childlike in her outlook and attitude about relationships, career and many other things in life. Most of this stemmed from the fact that she was unable to break free from the smothering influence of her mother and others around her who easily controlled her. She was always looking for external validation for the way she felt, acted and believed. Interestingly, Diane chose a career that depended mostly upon validation and approval from others: she was an actress who performed publicly. Her mother controlled Diane's professional life, telling her what roles to accept, where to perform and how to promote herself.

Over the course of 18 months, Diane slowly became aware of her innate ability to take control of her destiny. She realized that she had been terribly afraid of both failure and success, and that she had allowed her mother to take the responsibility for either turn of events. In this way, she had avoided claiming her independence as a separate person from her mother and at the same time, had given her mother what she wanted, which was to feel needed. In one session, Diane wondered if her guides and angels were helping her. Her spirit guides and angels were being supportive in every way, I assured her, but it was up to her to make changes in her life. She began to do so in small ways, such as purchasing a piece of artwork—

without her mother's approval—that she had admired for some time. Each time she did something in support of her own internal sense of self, she felt as if she had made a breakthrough. In time, Diane became much stronger in her ability to shift her locus of control from outside to inside of herself. She was changing the karma of the relationship with her mother and becoming much more balanced in the process.

The color that corresponds to the solar plexus is yellow and the musical tone is E. Compatible healing gemstones are amber, citrine, and topaz.

Questions and Exercises For Self-Enlightenment

1. In your journal, list several ways in which you claim your power in the truest sense. Is this in a career setting, in giving an opinion, or maintaining healthy boundaries in your life? How do you feel when you are able to claim your own power?

2. Do a brief meditation in which you see and feel yourself actively doing something that you have been afraid or reluctant to try. Examples may be speaking in front of a group, asking for a raise, or trying a new activity that requires you to step out of your comfort zone. Make it as real as possible, using all of your inner senses to really experience the moment. Affirm to yourself that you are allowing these changes to happen in your life now.

3. What does it mean to be your Authentic Self? How might you be more authentic? Do you find your career fulfilling? Are you able to express yourself in any given situation in a manner that is in accordance with who you truly are? Identify and list the blocks in your life that are standing in the way of achieving your vision for yourself. List at least one positive realistic action you can take to move through each block. Visualize yourself taking that action and affirm that you are in alignment with your right purpose now.

4. Write "power" affirmations on small pieces of paper that can be posted on your bathroom or bedroom mirror, or places in your home that you will see on a daily basis. Examples of these are "I love and honor myself exactly the way I am today," "I am worthy of all good things in life" and "I am comfortable with claiming my power and it feels good." Write your own affirmations; just remember to word them in

the present tense and with positive language. Remember to use "I am" when writing affirmations to claim the quality that follows them. Try this for one month and see how much more positive your thinking becomes.

7

THE HEART CHAKRA—LOVE

The fourth energy center is located in the center of the chest, near the breastbone. The heart, lungs, thymus gland, arms, shoulders, and diaphragm are located within the energetic domain of this chakra. In Sanskrit the heart center is called *anahata*, meaning, "unstruck" because it acts as a mediator in balancing the energies of the three centers that lie above and below it. It is the central passageway through which both earth and cosmic energies blend and are tempered from their "raw" state. Unconditional love, compassion, nurturing, and trust are all qualities that are experienced through the heart. When we block these emotions from flowing in our life, we may experience anger, resentment, bitterness, loneliness or hatred.

There are many imbalances in our consciousness that express themselves through the heart center. One of these is betrayal, which we are most likely to experience at least once during a lifetime. Betrayal in any form makes most people want to close the heart after having opened it in complete trust. It is only through the process of forgiveness that we can open the heart fully again. Sometimes this takes years and/or a physical illness or some other trauma to remind us of our inherent capacity to love and be loved regardless of the past hurt we have suffered.

Have you ever done something that your heart just wasn't in? On the other hand, have you done something you truly wanted to do with pure joy? Have you noticed the amount of energy it takes to do something that your heart doesn't fully participate in? We are doing ourselves no favor when we do something that is contrary to our true heart's desire because it creates conflict within us, which is an extremely draining energy to carry around. When the heart is "in" something, then *we* are. Too many people do not pay enough attention to what their heart is communicating to them. They would rather keep the job because it pays well, stay in the marriage because it's the "right" thing to do or adhere to a religion that no longer meets their spiritual needs because of family approval. In time, however, the heart always wins because it is the seat of our soul's consciousness and our inherent capacity to love.

There is something going on in the consciousness of a nation, such as the United States, where heart disease is so prevalent. In an attempt to pinpoint causes, many medical studies in recent years have pointed a finger at the nature of the American diet, coupled with a lack of exercise. Largely ignored until most recently have been the contributing factors of emotional and spiritual wellness and the role they play in relation to one's physical health. Over the past several years, however, there is a growing awareness among the medical profession that our emotions do indeed play a significant role in determining our physical health. Eastern cultures have known this for centuries and have realized the importance of incorporating mind-body practices such as yoga and meditation into everyday life, including the workplace. The importance of addressing and healing our emotions, especially stress, must not be ignored. Hopefully, American corporations will follow the example of their eastern counterparts and implement changes for both employees and management that will include stress-reduction programs.

Our collective consciousness as Americans was irrevocably changed during the terrorist attacks in Sept. 2001. As a result of this, we have been called to open our hearts in compassion and unconditional love to help one another and to realize the significance of world peace. As we continue to heal the grief, we are presented with the opportunity to allow our hearts to expand in a new direction. The Sept. events functioned much as a physical heart attack does; it caused us to reevaluate our entire way of being. Since that time, many people are taking the opportunity to shift their perception from the horror of the attacks to the revelation of what they are teaching us about our innate capacity to love, heal and forgive.

All of the great teachers, saints, and healers who have walked the pathway before us demonstrated the ability to create miracles of supreme magnitude by the mastery of their thoughts and beliefs. With even a subtle shift in our perception, we can open the gates to a new realm of being. In the great schoolroom of earth, we are often challenged beyond our most outlandish dreams to stretch our human boundaries of separateness and limitation. Each of us who has chosen to be on the planet at this time has made that choice based on exactly the experiences that our individual soul needs to advance spiritually. This is no accident. We are not victims of our circumstances, but masters of our destinies. The heart chakra continually teaches us flow and alignment with love, which is what we are here to learn.

Perhaps the biggest stumbling block that we encounter in following our heart's desire is that of distrust. This usually begins to occur by the age of six or seven. Young children are extremely trusting by nature, which is why they are very open to the world of spirit, seeing and hearing "invisible" friends that come to them. But when a child enters school and interacts more within society, he begins to shield himself emotionally for self-preservation. His home environment also contributes to the level of trust that is developed. Children who come from homes where there is substance abuse or physical battering usually have relatively low levels of trust. Often, they spend their entire adult lives attempting to regain a sense of trust in both themselves (since that was never encouraged) and the process of life in general. Sometimes people who have low levels of trust end up in relationships which tend to emphasize this imbalance by one partner becoming unfaithful. As a result, they become even less trusting and caught in a web of disillusionment about themselves and everyone around them.

Even in the best of circumstances, most of us suffer from a lack of trust in our own intuitive guidance. In fact, lack of trust in our own inner voice is the single biggest detractor from manifesting our purpose. When I teach intuitive development classes, I always ask at the start of the seminar why each person has come to the class. Invariably, people say that they want to be able to trust their own inner guidance to a greater degree. One woman said, "I receive the messages from the small voice inside me, but I find myself tuning it out. I need some sort of physical sign or something a bit more concrete so that I know I'm going in the right direction." Another explained, "I just don't trust my own judgment. That's why I go to a lot of psychic readers. At least then I know that I'm getting some advice that is more reliable." We all need confirmation from others at times, and occasionally a hand to hold. There is nothing wrong with wanting to get an opinion outside of our own. But sooner or later, we must learn to follow our own internal guidance and most importantly, trust that guidance to lead us in the right direction according to our mission and purpose in life. When we begin to follow our own guidance, regardless of mass or tribal consciousness, we flow in harmony and balance, which are also qualities that resonate with the heart center.

Another interesting observance I have made in teaching intuitive development seminars is that trust is built in stages. Typically, when people first come to the classes, they are contained within their barriers of distrust. This is reflected in their body language, posture and general demeanor. Before class begins, the room is noticeably quiet and there is little interaction among the participants. By the end of the second class, which focuses heavily on trusting one's inner voice of intuition, there is a noticeable change in the group. Bonding occurs within the group and deep friendships develop among classmates. One group that I taught bonded so completely by the end of the third level of classes that they exchanged phone numbers and agreed to keep in touch on a regular basis.

Opening our hearts to learn to trust again can profoundly transform our lives. Diane, a young woman who was about to enter a field of specialization in medical school, came for intuitive counseling sessions because she suffered from a complete lack of trust in her romantic partnership. Not only was she unable to trust that her partner was being faithful to her, she was equally unable to believe that the relationship was right for her. Time and again she would ask me in frustration, "Can't you tell me how he really feels about me?" Each time I responded, "What does he tell you when you ask him if he cares for you?" She would always reply that he did say he cared for her and, in fact, loved her. Clearly the issue was not if this man cared for her, but why she refused to believe him and trust in what he said. She continued to experience anxiety and panic over this relationship, believing it could end at any minute. I pointed out that this situation was showing her that she needed to open her heart and trust herself, regardless of what anyone else thought, even her romantic partner. She did not require his validation or anyone else's, for that matter, to exist and be loved. She admitted that for years she had struggled with a lack of trust in herself and the feeling had sometimes overwhelmed her, much to her detriment. She hated feeling so emotionally closed, not allowing herself to experience the joy of complete emotional intimacy with another person. Tearfully, she admitted that she had felt this way most of her life but didn't know how to change it. I suggested that she go back to the time in her life when she did trust, when she was a very young child. This she could do through recalling the Inner Child through meditation. By participating in past-life regression therapy, she could release and heal the wounds from lifetimes ago that had kept her imprisoned in grief. She agreed to consider it and began the journey of healing her heart. Although I haven't heard from Diane in some time because she went away to school, I know that she received the insights she needed to continue on her pathway of self-discovery.

Our innate capacity to love is something that we can all learn to express to a higher degree. Every time we are presented with a situation that calls us to open our heart a little bit more than in the past, we allow our divine consciousness to expand in new directions. Because we have forgotten our essential nature is love, we are continually in the process of removing the blocks to this remembrance. When we come to the physical plane, we are presented with opportunities that challenge our illusions about giving and receiving love. The vehicle of learning doesn't matter as much as the lesson. Our illusions are the beliefs that there are limited quantities of love, and that we will suffer from giving too much of it away. Yet our hearts tell us otherwise. In my work, I have learned that nothing is as crucial to our spiritual evolution as the ability to love. Although they say it in different ways, those who speak from the spirit world have consistently communicated this simple yet powerful message: Love is the only thing that matters.

Emerald green and pink resonate with the fourth chakra, and the key of F is the tonal frequency used to balance it. Healing gemstones are emerald, rose quartz, malachite and aventurine.

Questions and Exercises For Self-Enlightenment

1. Try this simple exercise. List in your journal as many ways as you can think of to define what love means to you. These could be one-word definitions such as "dog," "children," or "mother." After making your list, organize the definitions into categories such as "people" or "animals," "qualities that I define as loving," or "actions that are loving." Or make up your own categories. Under which group are most of your entries? What does this tell you about yourself and your life?

2. Close your eyes and focus on a positive quality that you want to experience more in your life. See yourself actively expressing that quality in as many ways as you can. Imagine how this would change your life. Record your experiences.

3. At least one day a week, do something entirely nurturing for yourself. Cook a favorite recipe, buy a single rose for yourself, or take time for a special activity that brings you joy. Celebrate the gift of giving and receiving within yourself. Also, allow someone to nurture you without feeling unworthy about receiving!

4. Never underestimate the power of making a gratitude list. Listing our strengths, blessings and gifts is always helpful in maintaining our perspective of just how much we are blessed. Add to the list relatives and friends, living or not, who reflect the qualities of love, trust or compassion to you. How have they shown this to you? How can you show this to others?

5. Is there someone you need to forgive? Try this meditation: Surround yourself in white light. Relax as you repeat a calming word or phrase in your mind,

such as "Peace", or "I am allowing Divine Spirit to heal me now." In your mind's eye, see the person you need to forgive standing in front of you. Surround this person in the same white light. Give thanks for the lessons. Release this individual to the healing light of God. Say aloud, "I release and forgive you, (Name). You are free and I am free. All ties that bind us in this energy are released and healed now." You may envision an energy cord going between you and the person, and it being dissolved as you say this. Repeat this meditation as often as you feel necessary, but know that healing has already begun on an energetic level the first time you did it.

8

THE UPPER CHAKRAS

The Throat Chakra—Expression

The fifth energy center encompasses the thyroid and parathyroid glands, mouth, neck, teeth, gums and ears Its Sanskrit name is "*vissudha*", meaning "purification." Energetically it is concerned with issues of expression and will. The throat center is our primary focal point for conscious alignment of our will with divine will. We are constantly making choices in our lives about how to use our power through the exertion of our will. Inevitably, we reap the effects of those choices. If our choice is not made in accordance with divine will, we may experience a problem or crisis in our life that points to the imbalance of our choice. Throughout life, we are constantly being reminded of the consequences of our choices. When we begin to align them with the highest intent, we flow in the harmony and balance of our purpose.

Our fifth chakra expresses life-force energy that we take in through the solar plexus center. To use this power in accordance with our soul's voice, we must allow it to be balanced through the heart center, which is the seat of our divine identity.

How often have you said something very cruel and immediately wished that you could take it back? This is because your internal sensor and balancer, the heart, spoke up on your soul's behalf. This is a literal energetic retraction that goes into effect and you may experience guilt as a result. It alerts you to the fact that you need to redirect your power of expression.

Anne came for an intuitive session in which she asked for guidance concerning her marriage. It seemed her husband, Jim, was routinely spouting off to her about incidental issues. He would be angry for a while and then go back to being his calm self. The session revealed that Jim hadn't been able to express himself regarding his job performance to a hard-nosed superior at work. Bringing the frustration home caused enough problems in the marriage for them to seek marital therapy from a psychotherapist. I pointed out to Anne that Jim was unaware of misdirecting his expressive power; he did not intend to be insensitive, yet he allowed his disappointments about work to control him. He was projecting his frustration onto Anne because he allowed his internal critic to be in charge of his personal power. Further, he was not tempering the frustration he felt by allowing himself to look at the situation through the balanced energy of the heart. Anne attracted his criticism because she was comfortable with expressing the role of the Martyr, and hardly took time to realize her own needs and speak up for herself. The combination of these patterns caused considerable strain on the marriage.

During our session, I suggested that Anne learn to nurture herself by creating an energetic return of all the energy she gave out. When we are giving out excessive amounts of our energy to others at the expense of our well-being, we end up feeling drained. By redirecting our energy to allow it to flow back to us, we can re-establish our power circuits and regain a sense of strength. This can be visualized by imagining a circle that flows around and through us, reconnecting us to our internal power. By taking time to nurture oneself in simple ways, such as spending time alone, engaging in activities that bring us joy and by spending time with people who validate our feelings, we allow the circle of giving and receiving to be completed.

Anne needed to set boundaries with Jim and others in her life, as far as what she would and would not accept from them. The session also made her aware of long-buried creative talents, drawing and painting, that were surfacing for her to express. I suggested she arrange time to speak with Jim about finding appropriate outlets for his feelings of frustration and make time to nurture her expression through her artwork. She left the session with a fresh outlook on how she could heal the situation.

The fifth energy center allows us to express soul qualities that have been developed and sustained through many incarnations. The soul's experiences are never lost or destroyed; they are always a part of individual consciousness. Submerged talents, abilities and experiences often surface when we align with our purpose and allow the full stream of life–force energy to flow through us. This is why so many people have "mid-life crises," which can be either life transforming or life shattering, depending upon one's outlook. A person's entire way of being may change as a result of facing and healing long-held blockages in the chakras. I have counseled women in their 40s and 50s who have had complete conversions in their personal expression. The loss of a spouse, a divorce, grown children leaving home or unfulfilled career ambitions are common launching points for major transition. Unfortunately for some people, a life-threatening illness is sometimes the wake-up call that signals the need to re-evaluate one's life and manner of personal expression. If we do not initially respond to the yearnings of our spiritual or emotional selves, we are likely to manifest a physical condition that provides the opportunity for us to recognize and heal our unbalanced issues.

Are you aware that your voice contains the essential vibration of your being? It is a resonance of the expression of your soul. This is how mediums can "read" people through their voice vibration over the phone. There are even methods of diagnosis for disease available now that use the voice to determine location and extent of imbalance within the body. Every time we speak, we are expressing our soul with its unique qualities. Consider how many positive ways the voice can be used: to heal, soothe, nurture, educate, entertain, laugh, greet and share. It can also be used to hurt, hate, shout, demean, insult, and condemn. Whatever qualities we choose to express, we will attract more of the same by virtue of the law of attraction. Just as our thoughts are magnets, our words contain the vibration of the intent behind them and will attract similar energy. The power of the spoken word is undeniable. This is why affirmations, positive statements of truth, can be incredibly effective healing tools.

According to the Hindu religion, God was first expressed as primordial sound. The syllable *OM* is the sound of original universal creation, and is chanted to call this energy forth. The *mantra*, a sacred word or phrase, has been used by millions of people during meditation and prayer. The mantra's power is in the unique combination of syllables contained within it. When it is chanted aloud, it is capable of attracting specific types of universal energy to the user. Similarly, every time we speak, we are sending out energetic vibrations into the universe that magnetically attract similar vibrations, which begin to gather and "stick" to the vibrations around us. Depending on the clarity of our intent and the emotional intensity that is behind our words, we will soon experience the repercussions of them. For example, have you noticed when engaged in an argument, your angry words prompt an equally angry response? In contrast, when someone speaks words of hope or healing to you, doesn't this make you inclined to return such qualities to this person?

In any relationship, communication is the essential ingredient that brings people together or pulls them apart. Are we encouraging or disparaging? Do we nurture or destroy with our words? Our tone is an equally important factor. Is it gentle or harsh? To discover this, tape record yourself and play it back. What qualities do you hear? This is what others around you are hearing. When engaged in conversation, are you an active listener? Active listening means that you can repeat to your partner exactly what was just said. The first step in effective communication is listening to what is being expressed. It is no coincidence that the ears and throat are connected by the Eustachian tube. Hearing and speaking are two sides of the same energetic function. We cannot do one without the other and hope to be an effective communicator, much less have harmonious relationships.

In childhood, many people have not been encouraged or supported in their personal expression, and have lost touch with their Authentic Selves as a result. This is particularly true with women. Dina came for a session because she had been unable to "find her voice" and experience fulfillment in her life. She was raised in a strict home and had been told the familiar adage "children are to be seen and not heard." She internalized this control and let it dominate most of her life. I couldn't help but notice she barely spoke during our session. Although an attractive woman, Dina projected an aura of uncertainty about her core identity. During the session, I was able to see that her problems with expression had originated in a previous incarnation in which she was ostracized from her family. She had been cast out for speaking up about deeply held religious views. It was utterly traumatic for her to be isolated from her family and the imprint of that emotion upon her soul carried over into her present life.

As part of her healing, Dina agreed to write and say daily affirmations. She was also able to see that she chose to be born into a family that discouraged her expression because she needed to examine and heal these old wounds by seeing them mirrored to her. As is often the case with human nature, if something becomes uncomfortable enough, we are forced to take a look at it. Dina saw the value in doing regression therapy to release the faulty thought patterns from her former life. I encouraged her to get in touch with the Inner Child by using a photo of herself when she was five years of age. She needed to talk to and validate the child who had not been encouraged to express herself. I also recommended that she speak into a tape recorder to reactivate the energy of the fifth chakra. By replaying the tape she could resonate with the vibration of her true voice and the power of her soul's expression that had long been silent.

The lessons of the throat chakra teach us, through the medium of language, to blend our human will with God's will. Because we have free will, we can change and redirect our power at any time. When we express our soul's innate capacity to love, forgive, and heal, and blend them with our personality and ego, we live and create our lives from a truly balanced perspective. To achieve this harmony, we must restore the balance in the fifth chakra energies by recognizing and claiming the power of our personal expression. We must take daily inventory of the manner in which we express ourselves and take steps to heal what doesn't serve us anymore. We must learn to listen to what we are saying and how we are saying it. Only then can we replace inauthentic ways of relating with fresh, positive ones that resonate with our highest intent and purpose.

An excellent healing gemstone that reflects the light blue color of the throat chakra is turquoise. Blue sapphire and angelite may also be used. The note of G in the tonal scale corresponds with the fifth center.

Questions and Exercises for Self-Enlightenment

1. How do you express yourself? In your journal, write a list of all your relationships. What is the quality of communication in each of these? In what way could you improve communication? List at least one positive step you can take to make improvements for each. How might you put these changes into effect?

2. Allow yourself to express your creativity in new and unique ways. Try a new activity that encourages you to be yourself without competition or judgment. This can be done alone or with a group. Allow yourself to play. Freeform dance, unstructured drawing and painting, or scrapbook–making can be outlets for your creativity and expression. Display what you make where you will see it daily as a reminder of your ability to create.

3. Facilitate a discussion group that encourages freedom of expression. Ideas for discussion are limited only by your imagination. In the last several years, the idea of forming spiritual book discussion groups has become popular. Allow equal time for participants to freely share their thoughts without judgment from the others. Have an open forum where a variety of topics are introduced around a central theme. Be aware of how you both speak and listen. What is your comfort zone for each?

4. Record and listen to the sound of your own voice. How do you feel about listening to it? If you had to describe the quality of your voice, what would it be? What does your voice reveal about your soul?

5. In your journal, write a few affirmations that emphasize a quality you want to embrace. Say aloud three times, putting emphasis on the quality of each.

Next, switch your voice emphasis to the "I am" in each affirmation. Notice how you feel when saying these. In what area of your body do you feel your power when speaking? In what area do you feel blocked? What is this showing you? Say the affirmations twice daily, in the morning and evening. Journal your progress.

The Brow Chakra—Inner Vision

Located in the forehead area, between the eyes, is the sixth chakra—*ajna*, which means, "to perceive," in Sanskrit. Physically, this center is connected to the brain, the nervous system, the pituitary gland, the eyes and the nose. Spiritually it corresponds to our consciousness of inner knowing, evaluation, truth and intellectual capacity. The brow's primary function is to perceive beyond the five physical senses. When it is developed, a person may experience clairvoyance and sense people, objects and occurrences that are above the physical threshold. The brow, which is also called the "spiritual eye," is the seat of our intuition and acts as a gateway to the perception of subtle realities and dimensions that lie beyond the physical.

As perfect children of God, we inherited all of the characteristics of our Heavenly Parent. These include the inner senses of clairvoyance (clear seeing), clairaudience (clear hearing), and clairsentience (clear feeling), which function independently from the artificial constructs of time and space. We have also inherited the ego, which is our navigator in the physical plane and director of most of our daily activity. In order to be balanced, we need to allow both inner and outer senses to develop in the highest possible way. As human consciousness continues to shift toward a higher vibration, we are becoming more aware of the need to use *all* of our senses and a higher percentage of our brain's capacity.

The brow center allows us to perceive the innate truth of our soul's purpose, and to use discernment in our thinking. It enables us to perceive beyond the illusions we have about others and ourselves, including the belief that we are separate from others. In the process of spiritual development, the sixth chakra facilitates our reception and comprehension of psychic information. When the brow center functions at its highest capacity, we have the inner knowing that surpasses logical explanation. The brow is called the "third eye," because it is the lens through which we see the reality of our spirit without the infraction of the personality and ego. Through it, we can see layers of our soul's reality that are not readily perceptible. From doing so, we can understand in the truest sense who we are and why we are here.

In teaching intuitive development, I have seen many people go through the process of opening the brow chakra to a higher degree. One of the most common things I observe is the relative ease with which most people clear and open this center. Because it is the seat of our judgment, the brow often becomes clouded with our negative assessment of others, our reality, and especially of ourselves. In order to perceive clearly, this energetic block must be removed. It is much like a cataract in our physical eye that clouds our vision and thickens over time until it is removed, permitting us to see clearly again. To remove judgment, I strongly encourage students to trust the perceptions they receive in the class development circles. Most of the time this is accomplished by receiving positive feedback and support about their intuitive impressions from each other during the classes. Interestingly, there always seems to be at least one person in every class who is convinced she does not have the ability to develop her intuition.

Claire is an example of one such student. One exercise that we use in class is to sense vibration from an object. This is called psychometry. It simply entails holding the object and allowing the description of people, places or things associated with it to come to mind. These psychic impressions can include colors, feelings and circumstances associated with the object. During the exercise, Claire became very anxious and expressed frustration that she "wasn't getting anything" from the ring that she was holding. I encouraged her to relax and trust her inner senses to allow them to open naturally. She became more frustrated. I then suggested that she start over, this time with a different object, an angel doll that another student had brought to class. I assured her that she could do this exercise; she simply needed to quiet the rational part of her mind that was telling her she couldn't do the exercise. Then I left her alone to do the exercise. When Claire rejoined the rest of the group, she had a huge smile on her face. As she shared her impressions of the angel doll, she was amazed when the doll's owner (another student) verified the accuracy of her comments. Among other things, she sensed that the doll had been given as a gift (the student's mother had given it to her) and had come from a far away place (Virgin Islands.) In this simple exercise, Claire learned to trust her ability to perceive beyond her physical senses. During the remaining classes, she continued to build on the foundation of trust she established in this session.

In recent decades, there has been much research and discussion about levels of human consciousness and the resulting implications for the individual, society and the world. Researchers who have attempted to locate areas of the human brain that are responsible for mystical and religious experiences found that we indeed have receptors in the brain for such occurrences. There have been numerous studies in recent years that have investigated near-death experiences reported by people from a variety of cultures and religions. Medical doctors, psychiatrists and psychologists are taking part in these studies as the boundaries between science and spirituality converge. We are increasingly aware that consciousness expands beyond the limited perception of the five physical senses and left-brain capacities. Our brow chakras are expanding to allow higher levels of spiritual consciousness to flow through us. Every time we release a limiting self-judgment, we allow more of our soul's unlimited potential to surface.

Miracles occur in our lives when we have a subtle shift in perception that allows us to experience greater insight into ourselves. Through intuitive insight, we can effectively evaluate areas of our lives, such as career choices and relationships. In order to accomplish this, we must necessarily admit to and break limiting ways of thinking and being. Each time that we choose to embrace our divine potential, we uplift the rest of humanity. When we make the choice to allow more light to enter our consciousness through the brow center—when we "en-light-en" ourselves—self-imposed barriers begin to fade to black. Then they disappear completely. When this happens, we enter a transitional phase in which nothing is the same as before. Some people may experience a sense of alienation from others, confusion, depression, and a general feeling of being disconnected. Our self-perceptions are uprooted when we begin to see through the clear vision of the third eye and become aware of our identity based on the truth within. Many ancient mystics, such as St. John of the Cross, experienced this dark phase on their journey to enlightenment. Jesus' temptations by Satan and his misgivings and fears before the crucifixion are also examples. When he confronted and released his fears, he ascended.

Every time we shatter a limiting belief about ourselves, we move closer to realizing the true nature of our soul. The more tightly we cling to our old belief patterns, the more painful it becomes to let go. Pain does not have to be a necessary ingredient in our spiritual growth; we can just as easily choose to learn through joy. Trusting and following our inner voice gives us the power to effortlessly release our self-judgments in love.

The sixth chakra gives us the gift of spiritual insight. We are able to see through the elevated perception of the spirit and not the illusion of the personality. From this vantage point we are afforded the opportunity to make balanced harmonious decisions. We can choose the best alternatives in accordance with our soul's purpose.

A woman in one of my intuitive development classes, Susan, a writer and poet, called recently to explain why she had not returned to class after two sessions. "I moved to Chicago," she explained. "I found myself getting on an airplane and flying to where I felt the most secure. My family is here, but the real reason I left was because I had a sudden and total awareness that I could no longer stay in a marriage that was built on a lie. I knew that I shouldn't have gotten married in the first place, but I allowed myself to believe in the illusion of it all. I decided to move in less than a week's time and am so happy I did. I have written ten songs since I left and am thinking about publishing them." She proceeded, "It was all because of the intuitive development classes that I had the realization to move." I knew that Susan was on the brink of making this life change and the classes simply allowed her to open her inner vision enough to make the right choice based on her needs. She shifted her perception enough to break through her denial about her marriage. At the same time, she had a burst of creativity in her writing that she had not experienced in a long while.

When the brow opens to a greater degree, we have a renewed sense of self, our talents and abilities. In childhood, our family may have told us myths about ourselves—such as we are stupid, unattractive, worthless, etc. If we internalized these beliefs, we grew up acting them out in countless situations that validated these opinions. Since like attracts like, the people, places and scenarios of our lives further substantiate these limiting perspectives of who we were. In the process of clearing the brow chakra, many people begin to see and fully understand their own truth for the first time in their lives. This can be exhilarating and frightening at the same time. The experience of increased creative flow can be exciting and rewarding, but the feeling of being rootless (without the support of the tribe) is not. We must allow ourselves to gradually adapt to the many changes that personal awareness brings with it and rest in the power of the moment. We don't always have to know the right answer instantaneously. Self-actualization doesn't happen overnight. Instead, we gradually move closer to realizing the Authentic Self, which does not support the limiting self-perceptions of who we have believed ourselves to be.

As mentioned before, the brow is the center for clairvoyance but is also partly involved in dream states and astral travel (the ability to move freely in fourth dimension consciousness). One indication that the brow is becoming more finely tuned is the ability to perceive astral colors with the inner eye. During meditative practices, the colors may come and go as the focus of this center shifts. Many children are clairvoyant because the brow is still relatively open from the soul recently being in the astral plane prior to incarnation. Around the age of seven or so, it begins to close, due to the child's need to conform to society and to peers. It remains unknown exactly how many children are truly clairvoyant, largely because of most people's hesitancy to discuss or give credence to it. Children who do experience clairvoyant abilities often keep it to themselves for fear of rejection from others, including their families. Those who are encouraged to speak openly about clairvoyance generally come from homes in which the parents are open-minded and/or already intuitively gifted. Perception of the spirit realm is not bizarre or frightening, but a natural, normal dimension of our existence. With familial support, children are more likely to grow up developing their clairvoyant abilities to a greater degree.

The color associated with the brow is indigo (purple-blue). The key of A resonates with this chakra, as do the gemstones lapis lazuli and azurite.

Questions and Exercises for Self-Enlightenment

1. What are some beliefs you have about yourself? These can be listed using "I am" sentences. For example, "I am successful at whatever I do." List both "negative" and "positive" beliefs you hold of yourself. Be honest when doing this self-assessment. How can you begin to shift your perception of the beliefs you desire to change? Think of at least one small step you can actively take to move toward changing your beliefs. How can you step out of the mold you may feel you are in?

2. Allow yourself to explore the possibilities of expanding and changing your beliefs through the powerful technique of visualization. See yourself acting, experiencing and being the person you desire to be. This could be as simple as performing an activity that you fear doing—such as speaking before a small group to share your ideas. See yourself being totally at ease in the situation. Practice daily— especially before going to sleep at night. Journal how your life is changing with the expansion of your beliefs of what you are capable of doing.

3. Meditation is an excellent way to increase your ability to focus your thoughts. If you are a beginner, choose a simple meditation in which you focus on color. Envision the seven colors of the chakra system from root to crown. Allow your attention to concentrate on the location of each center in your physical body and its corresponding color. Imagine that you are breathing in each of the chakra colors as you focus on that area of your body. Try to spend a few minutes on each one.

4. Monitor your daily thoughts and speech for self-judgment. Every time you catch yourself thinking

or saying something "negative" about yourself or another, change your train of thought with an affirmative statement that creates empowerment. Examples are: "I'm not going to put in for that new position at work. What's the use, I'm not really qualified for it anyway." Amend: "I am confident that the abilities I have are enough for the position I want. I am a qualified candidate for the job I desire now." To change your thoughts through visualization, imagine a blackboard in your mind's eye with the thought you want to change written across it. Now imagine a giant eraser sweeping across the board. Next, write your affirmation in large, red letters on the board and look at it. It only takes a moment to do this exercise and its impact is profound on your subliminal beliefs.

5. Think about the times in your life when you allowed your intuition to guide you, when you acted on a hunch or gut feeling. What were the particular circumstances? What was the outcome? How can you let your natural ability of insight come to the surface more easily?

The Crown Chakra—Purpose

The seventh center is located at the top of the head and is called *sahasrara*, which means, "thousandfold." It is often depicted in Hinduism and Buddhism as a lotus flower with many petals unfolding. The pineal gland and most of the brain, including the nervous system, are directly influenced by this center.

Our consciousness as spiritual beings is contained here in the awareness of our connection to the Divine. When we dream and engage in astral travel, the crown is the energetic portal through which we exit and enter. This is also true during meditative states, in which we experience union with higher states of consciousness. In a spiritually aware individual, the crown center spins at a heightened velocity. In an infant, the crown is relatively elastic, quite open and soft in the physical body (commonly called the "soft spot"). This is because the newly incarnated soul still spends time in the astral regions during sleep, using the crown as a doorway between the astral and physical worlds. As we mature, the crown generally becomes less open, yet more refined, especially if we practice regular meditation and prayer.

Many people have had the sensation of falling when they are just beginning to go to sleep. It feels as if something short-circuits and they are jolted back into their bodies. Also common is the sensation of spinning during meditation. Both of these phenomena are largely due to the crown chakra opening too rapidly, which leads to a mild temporary energy overload in the nervous system. With regular practice, the opening of the crown becomes modulated so one does not become overwhelmed during the process.

The seventh center also acts as our connection to the mind of God through the higher ideals of faith, inspiration and prayer. Each of these is so important to our existence as spiritual beings that they merit individual discussion.

Faith is belief in the unseen force of a higher consciousness that is constantly at work in our lives, guiding us in pathway of purpose. Depending on our spiritual beliefs, this higher consciousness exists within us, or in a separate Supreme Being that lives in the universe. In actuality, they are one and the same and there is no separation. Every time that we place faith in God, we place it in ourselves because we *are* God.

The histories of all major religions contain numerous examples of the power of faith operating in the lives of disciples. In Christianity, the parable of the mustard seed was used by Jesus to illustrate the strength of believing in the infinite power of God contained within us. There are numerous examples in the New Testament of individuals who were healed from illness and other conditions, such as demonic possession, because of their faith. When we seek union with the Divine, we invoke the energy of faith to open our hearts to an invisible yet powerful force operating in our lives. When we act in faith, we allow the hand of God to guide and lead us at every turn, no matter how much conscious objection our rational mind may give us. In my life, and in the lives of those around me, I have seen faith operating in magnificent ways with unbelievable outcomes.

As I shared in the first chapter, I am a member of a local metaphysical healing center started by three women who followed their dreams of starting a center with a strong emphasis on healing. On each anniversary of the center, each minister speaks of the dilapidated conditions of the building when they purchased it, and the enormous obstacles of its restoration. Because it is located in a conservative town that is home to many traditional denominations of churches, it has been difficult at times for the center to operate due to lack of community support. It has taken a large amount of faith to continue in the face of little positive cash flow, uncooperative neighbors, and extensive repairs to the building's structure. Yet the center continues to operate with a strong commitment to healing. Every time I hear the ministers speak of the obstacles they have had to overcome to make such a dream a reality, I am struck by the indomitable nature of our spirits when we allow faith to guide us.

Inspiration is the uplifting essence of divine mind merging with our human mind. It is what makes poetry beautiful, a thoughtful and kind word healing, and a summer sunset breathtaking. It is interesting that the word "inspiration" means "to inhale." Every time we are inspired, we are metaphorically breathing in the mind of God. Through this breath, we are refreshed and renewed by the elevation of our spirit. We can be inspired by the appreciation of beauty in any form, but particularly as it is reflected in the majesty of nature. One of the greatest inspirations of nature is the awareness of the continuity and cyclical nature of life as reflected in the four seasons. Countless writers and poets throughout the centuries have been inspired to write about the human spirit as it is reflected in nature. The natural intelligence and perfection of nature inspires us to trust in the ultimate perfection of our own lives, guided by the intelligence of the universe within us.

Another type of inspiration is the experience of being in what is called "flow." This is the complete merging of our mind with God's in which we release limitation, expectation and judgment. Dr. Wayne Dyer, author of numerous spiritual self-help books, refers to this moment as "sartori," which he describes as an "instant awakening." When we are in flow, we are completely in the power of the moment, able to see and feel everything from a sublime vantage point. We are not doing, we are *being*. Flow enables us to create and then detach from the outcome. This is when the canvas we are painting on becomes the masterpiece; the talk we are giving touches hearts and minds; and the household task we are doing becomes pure joy. Quite simply, to experience flow is to *become* flow. We are the painting, the talk, and the task. There is no separation between the experience and us. We are it and it is us. The miracle of our spiritual identity is revealed to us and we are filled with the realization that we are the expression of the Creator.

The most healing force in the universe besides love is prayer. Prayer is the concentrated focus of our good intent for another. Every time we pray for another with a sincere intent for that person's healing in whatever form it takes, we are uplifting our own vibration at the same time. Many times, prayer is all we can do in situations that seem relatively hopeless. More often than not, when we are able to remove our human judgment from the situation and release it to prayer, some form of healing occurs. Perhaps it is our shift in perception that allows this to happen. Equally important is our detachment from the outcome of our prayer. We do not know, or shouldn't presume to know, what another's greatest good is. An effective way to pray is to ask for the individual's highest and best good to occur, whatever that may be.

In my intuitive counseling sessions, I frequently sit with people who have gone through crises in their lives. For some, it is the serious illness of a loved one. A woman named Janet told me that her sister-in law, Ruth, had undergone treatment for breast cancer in the last several years and was currently in remission. Interestingly, as I sat with Janet, I felt that Ruth had experienced the effects of many people praying for her. I could sense a group prayer that had been directed to her. I asked Janet if she'd had any contact with a large group of people that would have offered such prayer. She replied that Ruth often watched television ministry and had sent in a prayer request for healing. Given the grand scale of TV these days, there could have easily been several million people who had prayed for her. The concentrated positive focus of so many people was likely enough to help heal Ruth.

Even a single prayer works wonders to uplift vibration. When a person is ill, his life-force energy has slowed to some extent. In a state of health, life-force energy flows through us easily and effortlessly. When we are emotionally or physically ill, the circuit becomes dulled or blocked. The act of praying helps to support the natural alignment of the person's life-force with that of the universe, which always seeks harmony and balance. Prayer puts us in direct alignment with the mind and will of the Divine when we remove our human will from the process and ask for only the highest and best outcome for the situation. At times, this may mean that a person passes on, seemingly unhealed from an illness. We must remember that this may be the very healing that needs to occur in order for this individual to continue the journey of healing in the spirit world.

How should we pray? All we really need to do is focus thoughts on the person and send love and positive intent for healing. Visualizing the individual in perfect health, happy and fulfilled, is extremely helpful. Because a photograph is a visual imprint of someone's energy, use of one in sending prayer can be effective. In addition, our name is our vibration captured in sound and can be said aloud as we send thoughts of healing to the person. Above all, prayers should be kept simple. Given the paradoxical nature of the universe, less is more and more is less. By releasing and detaching from the outcome of prayers, whatever the request, we can effectively allow the universe to work in its natural order, without the imposition of our expectations.

The seventh center connects us with our purpose in life. Knowing our purpose answers the question "Why am I here?" Coupled with this is the awareness of how we can use our talents and abilities to serve humanity. One of the greatest lessons of the crown is to teach us how to sublimate and balance the desires of the ego with the truth and integrity of God. This is similar but not identical to the lesson of the fifth chakra, which is the blending of human and divine will. The energy of the crown reveals to us the interconnectedness of all life and the ability to comprehend our universal citizenship. It teaches us to think, feel and act in terms of Christ consciousness, which is the perfect seed of the Father-Mother-God in each of us. Qualities that are reflected within this consciousness are selflessness, altruism and humanitarianism. In essence, it is the mind of God in all its totality within us.

As our collective consciousness continues to evolve, we are realizing how crucial it is to discover our sacred purpose. We are becoming aware how detrimental it is to our spiritual, emotional and physical well-being to remain disconnected from it. One of the most common reasons clients come for intuitive sessions is to gain insight about discovering and connecting more fully with their purpose. The first question I ask them to consider is, "What brings you joy and makes you feel alive?" Answering this brings us significantly closer to understanding why we are here.

Peggy was in the midst of a career change and finding her purpose in life. She asked what she could do to bring more spiritual awareness to her work as a personal coach and physical therapist. She was awakening to the idea of using energetic healing modalities in her work to facilitate quicker and more profound healing results. She wanted to know if incorporating these techniques into her work was indeed part of her purpose. In the session, she was given the confirmation from her guides to follow her intuition that told her to serve as a healing channel for others. She was encouraged to trust the innate sensitivity she had developed through years of helping people to overcome their emotional and physical limitations. Because she was connected to her purpose, Peggy was able to understand that her role in assisting people to heal encompassed more than just her initial training in physical therapy. This is why she chose to become a personal coach and holistic healer. Recently, Peggy developed a new energetic technique in her practice that promotes healing through release of blocks in the upper chakras. She was thrilled to assist people in using this technique and has reported great success in its effectiveness.

Often when we are in flow with our purpose, we experience the phenomenon of *acceleration* in our lives. Positive changes occur at a very fast rate in any or all areas of our lives. Doors open to us, synchronicities abound to connect us, and outmoded thinking patterns are healed. Our life circumstances change for the better. During these times of acceleration, we can experience the greatest rewards and hasten the process by letting go of resistance to change. We must necessarily release our expectations of how things should turn out, and allow trust to become our valuable ally. We must rely on our intuition, which is always the voice of the Divine speaking to us. We must allow the process of life to reveal to us the natural pathway of our heart's desires. It is through this journey that we can joyfully say "I AM."

The colors that resonate with the crown are violet and white. The tonal frequency is C. Two healing gemstones for this center are diamond and amethyst.

Questions and Exercises for Self-Enlightenment

1. In your journal, write the question "Why am I here?" Relax by doing a brief meditation. Ask to receive the answer to this question. Begin to write everything that comes to mind. Do not censor or filter your answers. Allow yourself to flow with what you are receiving. When you are finished writing, go back and read what you have written. What insights have you discovered about your purpose? If you have many, organize them into categories, such as "Emotions I Need to Heal," or "Abilities I am Developing."

2. Next, write at least one step you can take to realize your purpose. For example, if one of your answers was "to teach," list ways in which you are already doing this in your life. If you are not currently doing it, then list a way to begin. You may seek to teach in informal settings or one-on-one about your particular area of knowledge. Keep it simple; avoid listing expressions of your purpose that may currently seem overwhelming.

3. Begin to act on the steps that you have listed. Just because you are not ready to quit a job that you find unfulfilling doesn't mean that you cannot seek purpose through other avenues. Begin to seek resources, including people and organizations that are in accordance with your purpose as you see it. Find as many ways as you can to begin to speak and live your dream.

4. Affirm that you are in direct connection at all times with your purpose. A simple affirmation is "I am strongly united with my purpose now." Ask yourself the question, "How may I serve?" and listen to the answers you receive from your intuition. Remember

to remain open to the infinite possibilities of the universe. Answers may come in ways that you least expect and in divine timing, which is always perfect, although quite different from earthly timing.

5. Above all else, find purpose in what makes you truly happy. Purpose does not have to be on a grand scale; it may be as simple as caring for a pet, tending a garden or volunteering. Feelings of deep satisfaction are clear indications that you are meeting your purpose.

PART THREE

Receiving and Reconnecting

9

HOW THE UNIVERSE TALKS TO US EVERY DAY: SYNCHRONICITIES, SIGNS AND SYMBOLS

I was at the gym playing a game of racquetball when I received a call from my mother telling me that my father had died of a heart attack. His death was not unexpected, but it was sudden. I had seen him the previous night and he gave no signs of being distressed in any way. In fact, he died while on his way to work on Monday morning. His passing was that instantaneous.

As I got into my car and began to drive home, a certain melancholy twilight was falling. I felt strangely at peace, as my father had told me during a number of private conversations that he felt he was ready to go at any time, and probably would be going before very long. I was glad, in a way, to let him move on to the other side, to let him go and do what he felt that he needed to do there. I guess you could say, in a way, I was glad for him.

As I pulled onto the highway, I turned on the radio,

and I immediately heard the old Frank Sinatra song, "It Was a Very Good Year." My father had always been a big fan of Frank Sinatra, and I was immediately struck by the way that song seemed to fit that moment in time almost like a final, departing message. My father had led a turbulent life in many ways. He had a number of troubled, difficult times, but he had also been able to do a large number of very different things that affected the lives of other people in a very positive way. He led one of the most varied and interesting lives of anyone I have ever met. And just as the lyrics and the mood of that song went, I could almost see him talking about all of his greatly varied experiences, looking back and summing everything up. I'm certain that if I could have talked to him at that moment, this would have been exactly the spirit of what he would have said. He would have told me that his life had been full of learning experiences, some pleasant and some not so pleasant; but now that it was over and the journey had been completed, he could look back and say that it all fit together; that time had allowed everything he had been through to age in his soul like fine wine and he could say that, in the golden light of recollection, his life "poured sweet and clear ... It was a very good year."

—Joe Turiano

What is synchronicity? This story, submitted by one of the students who attended my intuitive development classes, is a good example of synchronicity and its impact on our spiritual understanding of life. In a nutshell, synchronicity is meaningful coincidence of two seemingly unrelated occurrences. From a metaphysical perspective, these occurrences can act as signs to us that we are one with the universe. Synchronicities are meaningful because they provide us with guidance, direction and comprehension in ways that we may not ordinarily receive. Our awareness of synchronicities is key in making these occurrences meaningful. The universe is constantly communicating to us if only we would pay attention. Synchronicities help us to open, comprehend and respond to universal communication that flows through our souls.

Recently, a friend and I were chatting on the phone about a new book that had been published. She was telling me how the author shared his personal stories of career disappointments, triumphs and climb to the top of his field. I was not aware that this book was on the market at the time. Three days later, I came home to find that very book lying on my dining room table. Apparently, my housemate had been in a bookstore and decided it would be something of interest to me. I hadn't mentioned the phone conversation with my friend. When I saw the book lying on the table, I knew that there must be some wisdom for me contained in the book because of the synchronicity that had occurred. Upon reading it, I discovered that I was experiencing some of the same struggles and lessons as the author. As a result of reading it, I have felt more inspired to continue on my life pathway.

Life is abundant with these little coincidences. There are no coincidences in life; everything in the universe has synchronistic meaning. Although the meaning may not be readily apparent to us, if we make note of it we can begin to experience a wonderful flow of communication with universal sources. We can then apply the inherent wisdom in these moments to expand our consciousness. Something as insignificant as hearing the same word or phrase repeated from different sources during the course of a week may offer us the opportunity to examine some aspect of our lives. For example, during the World Trade Center terrorist attacks, I constantly heard the word "freedom" used in both the news media and in personal conversations. During the chaotic and tragic aftermath of that time, as I would fall asleep at night I would sometimes clairvoyantly see the American flag waving clearly and brightly as I drifted off. As a result of this symbolism being communicated to me, I began to examine the meaning of personal freedom in my own life. I thought about restrictions, resistances and limitations that I had imposed on myself in an attempt to feel safe and to avoid certain responsibilities. This led to my thinking about how fear was still operating in my life and how I had allowed it to control me. With the awareness that had come through the symbol of the flag, I was able to make significant changes in my emotional patterns.

Another example of synchronicity is one that involves a friend's aromatherapy business. Vic recently decided to take on the responsibility of restarting his business of making custom-blended oils used for relaxation, massage and fragrance. With a major marketing expo coming to town in three days, Vic rushed to prepare his oils to exhibit at the show. He felt it would be an excellent opportunity to sell his products, reach new clients, and do something he genuinely loves. Because he had been out of the business for a long time, Vic experienced many doubts about doing the show. On top of this, he had little capital to work with and had spent most of his cash reserves buying the base products he needed to make the oils. Despite this, I could intuitively see that the art of making these oils was something Vic not only excelled at, but had brought him much joy and fulfillment. Several days before the show, we had lunch at our favorite Chinese restaurant. Vic wanted me to test the oils he had just made for the show. During lunch, he lamented how much money he had spent on concocting all of his products for the expo show. He wondered if he would recoup it. When we received our check, the waitress brought us the customary fortune cookies. Upon opening his, Vic started to chuckle. He handed it over to me to read the words, "All your hard work will soon pay off." We both laughed, as we knew this was a direct message from the universe that Vic was definitely on the right pathway and could release his worries. The weekend at the expo did indeed turn out to be a profitable one for Vic; he sold many bottles of oil and reached many new customers by networking and passing out flyers.

Many people have experienced the wonderful synchronicity of meeting someone in the right place at the right time. These meetings often act as catalysts in their spiritual and personal growth and provide opportunities for deep transformation. When these types of synchronicities occur, it is as if a powerful magnet has drawn the individuals together. Many of my clients have described meeting their spouse in this manner. Similarly, people have shared with me how they were magnetically drawn to certain spiritual teachers whose writings, workshops or classes made a significant impact on their lives.

Our spirit guides will often communicate an important message to us through the use of synchronicity to get our attention. Although these messages are commonly given for our spiritual growth and insight, some of them can be quite humorous. Several years ago, I met Herbert, one of my protector guides who regularly appeared to me in a full suit of medieval knight's armor. Soon after our initial meeting, Herbert communicated with me about some pressing emotional issues I was going through at the time. Because of the high moral code of ethics he had developed in his knightly incarnation, he also assisted me in understanding the value of discretion in communication, especially in mediumship.

One day not long after becoming aware of Herbert, I was driving down the highway and pulled up to a stoplight. I happened to glance over at the lane of traffic next to me. Just as the light changed, I noticed a large industrial truck roll by with a huge suit of armor, the company's logo, painted on the side of it. As I looked more closely, I saw that it was a truck belonging to a security company I had never heard of. I laughed out loud as I drove away, knowing it was a direct message from Herbert that he had somehow arranged for me to see. I realized it was his way of telling me he was watching over me. In all my travels since, I have never seen that particular truck or logo again.

The magic that synchronicities can work in our lives is directly dependent on our being open to them. We may have experienced the same occurrence before and simply were not open to receiving its message and meaning. It is helpful to record experiences of synchronicity when they happen to help us remember their special resonance with our soul. Keeping a journal reinforces the focus we place on these occurrences, thereby expanding their presence in our lives.

Symbols

Symbols can be defined as a visual shorthand for an idea, concept or feeling. Often they are universally recognized and act as a concise form of communication in a single image. Examples of symbols are everywhere in our culture, from the American flag to the Christian cross. Even our body language and facial expressions may be considered a symbol, as studies of body language have demonstrated the universal meanings of a smile and a scowl. Without saying a word, we can convey to those around us both positive and negative feelings through the symbolism of our body language, which speaks volumes about us and our attitude toward life. For example, when we are feeling defensive about a situation, we may unconsciously cross our arms across the chest in a protective stance. I have witnessed this in private intuitive sessions with individuals who feel threatened by the revelation of personal information. Most of the time they are completely unaware they are putting up this "shield" and often express disappointment when Spirit cannot penetrate the shield to impart healing messages. Even though I receive direct messages from Spirit, I cannot ignore someone's free will to be emotionally closed, defensive and block the information from flowing freely. In these instances, I suggest it is a good rule of thumb to remove all expectations before coming for another reading.

Spirits who communicate from the spirit world will often do so using symbolism. In many readings I have done, the client's loved ones come through and show me mental pictures of common symbols—such as a flower or bird—to communicate a particular message. One of the challenges of mediumship lies in the interpretation of these symbols, which can be ambiguous. Frequently the communicating spirit will use my frame of reference and experience to get across the idea. Then I have to communicate to the client what I am seeing and connect it to his or her life. It makes for some interesting and sometimes humorous times in the process! In many instances, the message can be heartfelt and reassuring—as in the session I had with Cara, whose mother kept showing me a beautiful rosebush in full bloom. Cara confirmed that her mother used to grow roses before becoming ill with cancer. But it was more than that. Cara's mother also was communicating feelings of unconditional love for her daughter and the immortality of the soul through the symbol of the rose. This was of great comfort to Cara who had not been able to find peace following her mother's passing because she couldn't let go of the grief she felt. Because she saw her mother suffer as she was dying, Cara worried about the process of death and especially what happens to us after we die. Her mother's message of love and immortality, encapsulated in the symbol of the rose, provided the healing that Cara needed to move forward in her life.

Many symbols are ancient in origin and depict powerful concepts in a simple image: the Egyptian ankh (the immortality of the soul); the rose (the heart and unconditional love) and the dove (peace, purity, and more generally, the Holy Spirit). Other symbols carry more complex and sometimes ambiguous meaning. The symbol of the snake can represent either primeval life force (yogic kundalini) or destructive impulses as in the creation story of Genesis. Similarly, the sword can represent both aggressive and destructive forces, or justice and divine truth. *

Recently, I experienced the powerful message of a special symbol that kept appearing in my life. A close friend had offered to do a written Native American totem card reading for me that would reveal the particular animal and insect guides that were assisting me in my present life pathway. I was intrigued to discover that the butterfly was a special guide in my life. The card reading talked about the stages of transformation in the life of the butterfly. I read it with some interest because it seemed to connect with changes I was experiencing at the time. About two weeks later I was sitting on my back porch talking on the phone when I happened to look down. There, close to my right foot, sat the most exquisite tiny butterfly with brightly colored dots of orange and yellow on its wings. Because the butterfly was currently out of season in my area, I had no idea where it came from or how it found its way onto my porch. Yet there it was, resting serenely by my feet, showing itself to me in all its splendor. Its size alone merited attention, as I had never seen one that small. I observed it that evening, and then tucked away the memory of its appearance in my life.

A few weeks later, I attended a healing exchange in which energy practitioners work on each other. When it was my turn to receive, I asked Tina—who was channeling the healing—for any particular messages she may receive for me. During the course of the healing she casually said, "I keep seeing butterflies around you. There are several of them, all different colors. Does that mean anything to you?" After I gave her confirmation of the recent appearance of the butterfly

---

* Definitions adapted from *The Dictionary of Symbols* by J. Tresidder, San Francisco: Chronicle Books, 1998

in my life, I felt certain that the message Spirit was revealing to me through the butterfly was the process of spiritual and personal transformation I was currently going through. The natural cycles of the butterfly's growth and eventual emergence from the protective chrysalis as a beautifully colored creature provided the perfect metaphor for my own emergence from the self-imposed cocoon I had wrapped myself in for many years. The message of the symbol was complemented by its simplicity, and I have thought about it ever since.

Colors and Numbers

Colors are symbolic because they convey essence, mood, and feeling by their appearance. Common interpretations for colors are: red—power and vivacity; orange—energy and warmth; yellow—cheerfulness and joy; green—harmony and life-force; blue—peace and healing; purple—insight and spirituality. The appearance of color in otherwise black and white dreams means we need to pay attention to what is being emphasized by the use of color; the subconscious mind often communicates an important message in this way. Visualizing colors in meditation is beneficial for connecting to and healing imbalances within the chakras. For example, to connect with the heart chakra, visualize bright green surrounding the breastbone. It is also helpful to "breathe" in the color and imagine it is penetrating the chakra being healed.

The symbolic significance of numbers is ancient, dating back to the time of Pythagorus, who was a mathematician and philosopher in the 6th century B.C. According to numerology (the influence of numbers on our lives), each number, from 0 to 9, corresponds to a specific vibration in the spiritual evolution of human and planetary consciousness. In various systems of divination, including the I Ching and the Tarot, numerology is used in the interpretation of the spread.

Because numerology works with only single digits, a double-digit figure is added together to calculate a single number. For example, 11 in numerology calculates to the number 2 by adding 1+1.

Numbers are symbolic because they communicate complex ideas in a consolidated form. The common interpretations of each number are: 0—pure potentiality and possibility; 1—initiation; beginning of a cycle; 2—balance, harmony, duality, and relationships; 3—joy, creativity, groups and self-expression; 4—foundation, security, structure and stability; 5—adaptation, challenge, competition and change; 6—peace, calm, contentment and family; 7—spirituality, introspection, study and solitude; 8—order, recognition, power and material satisfaction; 9—end of a cycle, completion, fulfillment, and forgiveness.

Any set of digits, no matter how large, can be added and reduced to a single digit for interpretation in the numerological system. For further explanation of numerology, including your personal life path number, see *Tarot, Plain and Simple* by Anthony Louis (Llewellyn Publications, 1996).

Understanding symbols in the process of our spiritual growth is invaluable because in many instances, the universe will use symbols to communicate complex ideas. I believe this is so because there are layers and depths of meaning communicated to our souls in ways we cannot even imagine. Although we are not always able to grasp the meaning of a symbol on a conscious level, our soul is deeply aware of these occurrences and interprets them in the unspoken language of universal comprehension.

Archetypes

Universal archetypes (ancient thought patterns and models deeply imbedded in our subconscious) are another form of universal communication that can relay much information to us in a single image. Examples of archetypes are those of the mother, the father, the hero, the savior and the warrior (see the energetic archetype glossary for definitions of other archetypes.) Throughout human evolution, we have held such strong thoughts and beliefs about certain people and concepts that the thought patterns associated with them have become an innate part of our subconscious. The renowned psychologist Carl Jung studied archetypes and their relationship to our lives. He believed they existed from culture to culture, and were often depicted in our dreams, myths, and fantasies.

A pictorial representation of some archetypes is found in the deck of 78 Tarot cards, which may be used for insight and guidance in one's life. Originating in the early middle ages, the cards were first used as a game before later becoming a tool for divinatory practices. The 22 major arcana cards are used to symbolize common universal archetypes in human consciousness, beginning with the Fool (potentiality, innocence) and ending with the World (completion, success, fulfillment.) The particular selection, layout and numerology of the cards used in a Tarot spread reveal how subconscious energies are operating in the user's life. They may also indicate the probable outcome of a given situation if the questioner remains on his or her current pathway. The use and study of the Tarot is an excellent way to learn about how archetypes integrate with and operate in one's life. The resulting spiritual insights can be quite illuminating when we employ them.

Understanding the Messages of Symbols

To avoid confusion and understand the meaning of symbols, it is best to interpret them in their simplest form. When you become aware of a symbol that appears to speak to you in some way, it is usually beneficial to accept the meaning that is most obvious to you. Avoid overanalyzing. It is also beneficial to jot down or sketch your symbol for further clarification. You may dream of or have future identification of the same symbol.

Have you ever considered how a single day is symbolic of the pattern of your overall life? Take a moment to consider how your time is spent each day. Do you spend your time in "other"-directed activities such as care-taking? Are you consumed by "doing" versus "being?" Do you allow the mechanics and structure of everyday life to keep you from pursuing more purposeful and meaningful activities that would enrich you? Are you constantly on the go, never taking time to quietly go inward and receive guidance? How is your home symbolic of who you are? When we begin to examine the content and fabric of our lives, we can facilitate the process of change in our spiritual growth.

In addition to looking to our daily routines for symbolic meaning, we can consider the world of nature, which is replete with rich reflections of our human nature. The seasons are deeply significant in the understanding of our soul's journey. Each season evokes a reflection of our own internal cycles of birth, growth, death and eventual spiritual maturation and contains abundant illustrations of how to adapt to life's inevitable changes. In the wildlife kingdom, animals are symbolic of our personalities; sometimes humorous and playful, other times predatory, uncompromising and territorial. For centuries, poets and writers have looked to the symbolism of the natural world for inspiration and guidance in countless ways. We too, can connect with and spend time in nature, even if it is only our own back yard, to find renewed strength and inspiration to continue our earthly journey. The perfection and timelessness of nature provides us with the perfect lens through which we can view the immortality of our own soul.

The key to understanding how symbols speak to you is simple awareness of the things you commonly take for granted. Symbolic meaning is contained within the words we speak, the streets of our hometown and the furnishings of our homes. Everything in our external environment is a reflection of the internal condition of our souls, and serves to remind us of the unity of all creation. When we become conscious of the messages that symbols offer, we can better understand our world, our lives and ourselves.

Questions and Exercises for Self-Enlightenment

1. Take a moment to think of a symbol that has special meaning to you. If you can, draw it in your journal. How does it speak to you? What are the layers of meaning behind it? How does it relate to your life? Write your insights.

2. Take a quick look around your living environment. What are the colors that surround you? Are they earth tones? Bright or calming hues? How do they make you feel? Now notice the objects and furnishings of your environment. What messages are these communicating to you? If the objects could talk, what would they say? In what way are your furnishings symbolic of your life?

3. For one day, pay close attention to the words expressed in conversation with others. What do they reveal to you about yourself, your attitude and your life? How are your words reflective of your emotions? Throughout the day, is there a particular word that keeps resurfacing in your interactions with others? In what you are reading? What could the meaning of it be for you?

4. Take a walk around your yard or your favorite place in nature. Let your senses envelop you as you walk or sit quietly. What facets of nature do you connect with first? Explore the area visually. What draws your attention? Are they colors, sounds, animals, trees? What is the symbolism contained within this as it applies to your life now?

5. How have you experienced synchronicity in your life? Have you met someone by magical circumstances? How has it changed your life?

10

Going With the Universal Flow: How to Attract Abundance and Prosperity

O ne of the most magnificent qualities of our universe is the limitless abundance of the Creator. Given our inherent divine nature, all we need do is ask and open our hearts to receive a bounty of universal creativity, wisdom, healing and love. In a utopian world, we would all be richly abundant in every facet of what the universe has to offer. Lack, poverty, illness and war would not exist because we would realize that each of us has the ability to manifest perfect health, loving relationships, rewarding careers, and anything else we desire. Each individual would realize that he or she already possesses the innate ability to create fulfillment and happiness. We would come to understand the natural workings of the universe, where the energies of balanced giving and receiving are the keys that allow abundance and prosperity to open and flow forth. Further, we would know that every word, thought or deed that had love as a basis would never be ill spent. We would claim abundance and prosperity without allowing guilt or low self-esteem to block us from receiving it.

Of course, we do not live in such a society today. Instead, we live in a world that believes in and supports the ideas of lack, poverty consciousness and luck. We live in a society that embraces class systems that divide us into "Haves" and "Have-Nots," based on our income levels and material possessions. Thankfully, more people today are becoming aware that abundance and prosperity are more than abstract concepts that are totally unattainable for them. Increasingly, we are beginning to understand that how much money we earn and the state of our financial affairs is a direct reflection of the thoughts, beliefs and spiritual consciousness we hold. We are learning to accept the fact that prosperity is directly affected by one's attitude towards life in general, and has little to do with actual material resources. Authors such as Suze Orman and Shakti Gawain have done much to educate people about the emotional and spiritual aspects of money. With the realization that prosperity is more than a matter of how much material wealth one has, we are beginning to understand our relationship with money in a new light of spiritual and energetic dynamics.

Prosperity encompasses far more than our monetary or material possessions. We may have little money in the bank, but be richly abundant in other ways, such as having good health or close friends. Prosperity is an entire way of being that focuses on our ability to believe in the infinite resources of the universe. It is the belief that whatever we need in life is already being supplied to us in limitless quantities. Most importantly, it is the belief that the power resides within us to manifest whatever we want in life.

Giving and Receiving

Everything in our lives is a reflection of the particular beliefs we hold. The amount of prosperity we experience in our lives is directly related to the thoughts we have about giving and receiving. The interrelationship between these two vital energies (giving and receiving) can easily be depicted in the shape of the circle, which has no beginning or end. The law of karma tells us that what we put out into the universe will eventually return to us. Whatever we give, we will also receive. Elements of time and form are the only variables in this equation. That is, we don't necessarily know when or how the given energy will return, even though we know that it will. If we desire to strengthen our relationship with prosperity, we need to examine the balance of giving and receiving in our lives. Many people have difficulty in maintaining equilibrium between these two energies. To examine how these energies are operating in our lives, it is helpful to look at our core attitudes about them. Let's first consider the beliefs that were passed onto us from our family.

When we begin to examine and heal our beliefs about prosperity and money, we must look at our childhood beliefs. Some people have grown up with the belief that there is never enough to go around. This is a belief in lack, quite the opposite from a belief in abundance. Their family may have worked very hard to get ahead, only to continuously come up short in the financial department. Or the family may have believed that it is necessary to compromise by giving up something in order to get something else. Also common in many families is the belief that some people are just lucky, and that is why they have more. Another belief is that "fate" or external sources determine how much money one has. Although none of these beliefs are true, it is the power we give them that enables them to keep us bound to a limited view of prosperity. As soon as we begin to change our thoughts about what is possible for us, we begin to heal and reinvent our relationship with prosperity, abundance and money.

The universe provides us with the amount of prosperity that matches our beliefs about how much we are willing to give and receive. This applies not only to material items, but our time and physical energy as well. If, for example, we were taught that it is better to give than to receive, we will eventually feel depleted, drained and short-changed. This is a lesson that many people learn when they constantly take on too many responsibilities, often at the expense of their emotional and physical health. Sooner or later they discover that the price they pay for giving too much is excessive, and they must learn to receive by accepting help from others. On the other hand, if we allow ourselves to become entirely self-centered and can only take from others, we eventually succeed in pushing all forms of prosperity away from us because we are not completing the energetic circle by giving. In the 12-step program of AA, there is a slogan, "You've got to give it away in order to keep it," which refers to the practice of maintaining sobriety by sharing one's experience, strength and hope with other members. This can be applied to the concepts of abundance and prosperity as well, and is another one of the spiritual paradoxes that often confound us until we begin to comprehend the nature of the universe.

Blocks in our Thinking

There are many ways in which we prevent the full abundance of the universe from manifesting in our lives. It is important to understand that most of these blocks reside in our subconscious minds. Because the subconscious accepts whatever information is put into it, it is possible to release and "rewrite" patterns of thinking that create our experiences. Even if we have held a pattern for many years or lifetimes it can be changed. As with any type of healing, our core ideas must first change before we see tangible results in our lives.

In addition to our family's beliefs concerning prosperity, we may harbor feelings of unworthiness regarding our ability to use our natural talents to their best use. When this occurs, we never allow ourselves to receive the magnificent blessings that come with following our inner voice. Or we may believe that if we do succeed in life it means we will move out of the comfortable space we have been in. This is the much talked about "fear of success" syndrome that keeps us stuck in the same position for years, despite our innate sense of the need to move on. Both of these imbalances in our thinking stem from a block in the third chakra, which is the seat of our personal power.

Sometimes we are afraid of giving too much because when we have done so in the past, someone has taken advantage of us. We may close our hearts to the idea of giving and block ourselves from experiencing the joy that comes from giving without expectation. Closing our heart prevents our life energy from flowing outward and denies us the opportunity to adequately receive in turn.

Another block that prevents us from receiving is feeling unworthy. In this case, we do not allow ourselves to receive fair compensation for our work, gratitude for our time, or material gifts for just being who we are. I have known individuals who manage to successfully block every form of exchange possible for their investment of energy in a project because they don't feel worthy to receive. Over time I have watched them become angry, tired and resentful because of the lack of sufficient return for their efforts. Like the "fear of success" syndrome, the inability to receive is due to deep feelings of never "measuring" up to self-imposed ideas of perfectionism and to fear of loss of control. Individuals who have this block may feel as if they are under the control of the "giver" and have lost their autonomy. They often give their time and talents away because they want to avoid feeling out of control or obligated.

Rhonda was at a loss to understand why she always felt unappreciated by her superiors. In our session, she inquired about her chances of moving up within the organization. She was constantly overlooked when it came time for a raise or promotion. It became evident during the session that Rhonda believed she was not worthy to receive any more compensation for her work than she was currently receiving. Deep inside, she feared that if she were to assume a position of higher authority within the company, she would lose the security of the life to which she had grown accustomed. This included friendships with others in her department that she believed would dissolve due to jealously over her promotion. She feared that others wouldn't accept her anymore. I suggested that Rhonda begin to look at the restricting beliefs she had surrounding power and achievement and how they blocked her from realizing her goals. I suggested she work with affirmations and subliminal tapes to "re-program" her subconscious mind. The next time I saw her, Rhonda's beliefs about her self-worth and ability to handle success had begun to change. As a result, she soon received a promotion and a raise.

People who take far too much responsibility for the happiness and well-being of others also unwittingly block themselves from receiving abundance. Content to play the role of the Martyr, they send a powerful message to the universe that others deserve to receive love but they do not. They are also saying that others are not capable of managing their own lives. In this way, they create an unbalanced situation in which both parties are blocked from the circle of prosperity. Often the need for external approval is at the heart of this block, which emanates from the power center of the third chakra. Taking too much responsibility can likewise indicate a need to control others so they will put us on a pedestal and build their lives around us. After all, how could they possibly survive without us?

Another block that prevents us from claiming abundance is one that concerns our unique circumstances in life. We may believe that our "destiny" in having abundance and prosperity is automatically determined by our educational level or gender. Examples of thoughts that are at the core of this belief are, "I'll never get the job I desire because I'm not educated enough" or "I won't get approved for the loan because I'm a single woman." Also destructive to allowing the flow of prosperity is the belief that ethnicity precludes us from receiving all life has to offer. Unaware that this belief keeps us safe from stepping out to receive, we allow anger and blame to block us from claiming prosperity. We may feel it is easier to reject abundance than deal with the inevitable changes it creates in life. Despite the security of these childhood beliefs, they are extremely limiting and counterproductive to our spiritual growth in the long run.

As you can see, there are many ways that we can deny ourselves prosperity, all of which are a direct result of our limited thinking about the abundance of the universe, the fundamental laws of giving and receiving, and our own divine nature— including the ability to manifest whatever we want. The good news is that we can heal our thoughts and begin to open to the flow of prosperity that becomes ours for the asking.

Opening to the Flow of Abundance

There are several crucial changes in our thinking that must be made to allow abundance and prosperity to flow into our lives. In examining our long-held beliefs about our sense of worthiness and how natural laws governing the universe operate in our lives, we may realize that we have been blocking ourselves in fundamental ways from receiving. When we embrace the belief that we are deserving of the best life has to offer, we are well on our way to realizing how the universe can work with us in providing all we need. The following are some ways in which we can begin to change our thinking about abundance and prosperity.

First, we must accept the belief that the universe is a storehouse of infinite energy that is at our constant disposal.

Much like a computer, it responds with an output that directly matches our input. In essence, we must tell the universe specifically what we want in order for it to respond to our specific need. How do we know what we really need or desire? Many people discover they unintentionally attract a situation that they did not really desire. The old adage, "Be careful what you pray for" illustrates this point. A good way of making certain that we draw to us exactly what is in accordance with our divine purpose is to set our intention for the very highest and best situation possible at any given moment. By doing this, we eliminate our ego's part in the process. During the times we find ourselves standing at a crossroads in making major decisions, we need to ask ourselves this question: Which choice (situation) brings me closer to my sacred purpose? We will receive the answer to this question through gut feelings, interaction with others in our life, or synchronistic events. If we set intention based on our soul's purpose, we will be in accordance with the highest energy available to us.

We must also align our beliefs with faith in all of our daily dealings, no matter how insignificant. We need to have faith not only in the limitless abundance of the universe, but also in the Divine, who is meeting our every need at this *very moment*. We must focus our attention on the power contained within the present moment. By keeping our thoughts and energy in the present, we allow more flexibility in the process of manifestation. Remember that patience is necessary when we are learning any lesson, and this is especially important because we may not see immediate tangible results of our change. The element of time is needed to allow the particular circumstances we desire to manifest.

It is very important that we cultivate gratitude for all that we already have in our lives. When we are grateful, we reinforce the energy of abundance. Since our thoughts create everything in our lives, feelings of gratitude will attract similar thoughts and experiences to us. Nothing is too small to be grateful for—including clean water, healthy food, and the place we call home. Lately, I have become very aware of the need to express thanks for a strong, healthy physical body. Each morning when I exercise, I say, "Thank you, Divine Spirit, for the magnificent vehicle of my physical body that has enabled me to come here and learn my spiritual lessons." Our bodies have an innate intelligence and respond to the energy of unconditional love. What we focus our energy on expands; giving thanks reinforces and multiplies what we are grateful for.

Too many times we allow anxiety about our conditions of lack, whatever they may be, to dominate our thinking. Every time we concentrate on what we don't have, we attract more of the same into our lives. To break this cycle, we must shift our focus onto all of the good things, people, and situations that are with us at the moment. On a daily basis, we need to acknowledge everything that is "right" with us and give heartfelt thanks. It is possible to express gratitude for the lessons we have learned through "wrong" choices or situations, as well. During the last year, I have become increasingly aware of the shifts that occur in my life when I give thanks for situations that I have perceived as unpleasant. I have come to understand that *everything* and *everyone* in my life teaches me about myself in some way. When I allow my thoughts to be filled with gratitude for these situations, my life becomes easier as a result of releasing anger, resentment and fear.

Desire is a necessary element that allows manifestation to occur more rapidly. Desire is the energy of soul "fire" that emanates from within us (see "The Power of Thought: How to Affirm Through Desire and Intent). Generally, the stronger our desire, the quicker results appear from universal sources. Intent is the other important element that is a part of manifestation, which is the focus of our thoughts on a specific outcome. We should be specific about what we want, but remain flexible enough so the universe can use all sources to bring us what we desire. Amazing miracles occur when we remain open. Our guides and angels can assist us in ways that we cannot imagine if we are open-minded enough to allow them. For example, if we are seeking employment, we may be prompted by our guides to go to a particular place or meeting where we encounter someone who offers us a job. Or we may be in the right place at the right time where we hear of a job opening.

Remember that our guides and angels always work in accordance with our free will. They are our companions who can see the big picture of our lives and help us to connect to our soul's purpose. They are aware of the infinite possibilities of the universe and make every attempt to assist us in our spiritual growth. This does not mean that we sit back and do nothing. It *does* mean that we must do our part in moving forward on our pathway, yet remain fully open to their assistance.

De-Clutter!

To assist in the process of manifestation, it is extremely helpful to clear out as much clutter as possible from our lives. This consists of releasing physical debris as well as emotional and mental baggage that no longer serves us. We may have to do a good, old-fashioned spring cleaning to clear the way for prosperity. Getting rid of anything that is not useful and donating it to a charitable cause is an excellent way of clearing our space to allow fresh energy to enter and circulate. It also opens and reinforces the circle of giving and receiving that completes the circuit of abundant flow in the universe. Overall, the simpler we can make our lives, the better. Energy flows much more harmoniously in the absence of clutter and can return to us at an accelerated rate when we are in a clear space, mentally, emotionally and physically.

To get rid of emotional clutter we must begin the process of forgiveness. When we do this, we must remember to first forgive *ourselves* of any perceived wrongdoings. Too often, people skip this step and rush into the business of forgiving others, only to discover that old hurts and regrets resurface. In forgiving ourselves, we must develop the understanding that we are here to learn, grow and stretch spiritually. We would not have made the decision to come here if we did not want to grow! The challenges we experience along our pathway are necessary for us to see the light within, and we need to view *all* of our experiences through the eyes of our soul, which does not judge.

A simple ceremony of release may help to finalize the process of emotional clearing. To do this, write on a piece of paper who or what you wish to forgive and then burn it. When burning the paper, you can say an affirmation such as, "I am releasing and forgiving (name of person) for our highest and best good. I send all past wounds, hurts and grievances that I have been carrying to the light for healing. I am free and you are free. I release and I forgive all who have hurt me. I send them unconditional love for their journey." This forgiveness exercise can be done even if the person who hurt us is no longer in our lives. He or she may even be in the spirit world. When we forgive, we do so from a soul level, which means that we do not have to connect with the other person physically or emotionally.

I cannot emphasize enough that the act of forgiveness is the single most important factor in freeing ourselves from the limitation of poverty consciousness. It greatly enhances the ability to be a channel for the flow of universal abundance when we clear out agendas of fear and emotional pain that have blocked us for so long. At the same time we release these perceived hurts, we release the victim mentality that accompanies them and prevents us from claiming abundance. The truth is that each of us has the ability to bring into our lives whatever we desire, regardless of the past. The more we are able to release our limitations of past baggage, the more we open ourselves to receiving the gifts that are rightfully ours as divine beings. Remember the saying, "To err is human, to forgive is divine?" Every time we forgive, we do so from the highest part of us, which is the Christ Self (the perfect reflection of God within humans.) This means that we release our ego's need to be right, to be in control or to win. We understand the spiritual lessons in any given situation and give thanks for their presence in our lives.

Besides clearing our emotions through forgiveness, it is helpful to release any people, places or relationships in our lives that drain us emotionally. This includes people who are energy "vampires." When we are in contact with someone such as this, we end up feeling depleted and tired, even after the person has left. It is up to us to set our emotional boundaries in these instances because most energy vampires are not even aware of what they are doing. Certain places can also drain our energy and reinforce a sense of poverty consciousness. I have found that the energy of bargain retail stores, nightclubs, and certain areas of town can have a negative effect on my energy level. The thoughtforms that are associated with these areas are not always of the highest vibration and may actually lower our personal vibration if we stay in them for too long. It is helpful to cleanse our auric field by visualizing white light after leaving these places.

The Courage to Quit

In my practice of counseling, I have met many people who have sought guidance on manifesting a more fulfilling career. Rosemary, an attractive woman of 45, worked for a large corporation for five years. Although she was making a handsome salary, Rosemary was desperately unhappy with her position because she was extremely burdened with the amount of work she was required to do. More than that, however, was the fact that Rosemary did not agree with the ethics of her corporate management team. The company had some unscrupulous business dealings and expected Rosemary to go along with the deceptions. On top of this, she felt ill most of the time and dreaded going into work in the morning. Her family had suggested she look for employment elsewhere, but Rosemary persisted in her current position because of the huge salary. She felt that she would be unable to find a job that would pay her as much. During the session, it became apparent that Rosemary needed confirmation that she needed to move on. It was clear this job was killing her spiritually, emotionally and physically. I suggested that she look elsewhere and ask the universe to supply her with a more suitable position that would be in accordance with her purpose, using her abilities and talents. Formerly, Rosemary had taught at a university and written freelance articles for publications.

Eight months after our meeting, Rosemary came for another session. The first thing I noticed about her when she walked in the room was her overall demeanor and the strength of her aura. Gone were the worry lines from her face. Her smile was bright and clear as she announced, "I quit that job and went back to my first love, teaching. It is the best thing I could have done for myself." She added that she knew she had to let go of the job because of its effects on her health. She also realized that she had manifested the lesson to learn about her need to remain true to herself, despite how much money was involved. It became clear that this pattern was one that Rosemary had faced before and was a karmic lesson she had agreed to learn. Switching jobs probably added ten years to Rosemary's life.

I have advised many clients like Rosemary to *never* do anything just for the money. Every time we do something we don't really like merely because it pays well, we compromise our integrity and send a message to the universe that we are settling for less than we deserve. What we deserve is a career that we love and that answers to our purpose for being here. The adage, "Do what you love and the money will follow" speaks about the need to satisfy our spirit's passion, whatever that may be. Each of us has unique innate talents and abilities that can be used in a variety of ways. Opening to the abundance of the universe means that we allow these abilities to be expressed to their highest degree. The expression of our spirit is necessary for us to be in a state of complete harmony. The Divine's plan for us has *never* included the intent to labor at boring, meaningless work that depresses our spirits, simply to get by in life. Why then, do we continue to do it? Do we really want to end up like Rosemary—emotionally depleted, unhappy and on our way to manifesting physical disease?

In seeking employment, we must ask ourselves what makes us feel alive and full of joy. What makes our soul sing? What gives us the feeling of internal satisfaction? I advise people to write the answers to these questions and begin to look for employment in accordance with these qualities. This is finding "authenticity" in livelihood. To be authentic is to be real. To be real is to listen to the voice of the soul. When we are following our soul's desire we are on the pathway of creating prosperity.

Tithing

One of the most powerful magnets for prosperity is the simple act of tithing, which is the selfless giving of some of our resources to a person, organization or cause. In any instance of giving with an open heart to benefit others, we connect with abundantly powerful energies that are associated with prosperity. These include selflessness, belief in the abundance of the universe, altruism and generosity. Tithing expands our personal life-force energy up and out, which can be visualized in the shape of the *spiral*. Because money is a material representation of an energetic exchange, it is possible for our money to represent our energy in situations in which we aren't directly involved. The value of tithing is its capacity to touch many people, causes, and animals that are beyond our direct sphere of influence.

Whenever we give money, material goods, or time, an energetic pathway is set up that is circular in nature. The energy we have given, in whatever form, will be returned to us. Because of the law of karma, there are no exceptions to this. Depending upon the intent surrounding it, this energy may be multiplied many times upon its return to us. This usually happens when we give with a pure heart, without expectation of return. The vibration of love that surrounds our giving expands and intensifies the energy. In fact, there really is no sense in giving if it is not done from a loving basis. I have observed that most, if not all, successful people regularly tithe to charitable organizations. I have also met people who could not really afford to tithe, but did so anyway. It is their belief in the limitless love and abundance of the universe that has enabled them to do so. I knew a friend's aunt who often gave to people in need of food, clothing and money. Although she did not have much money herself, she always gave with an open heart. Today she is in her eighties and often says she has been richly blessed by the "good Lord" who has never let her go without. She is a woman of tremendous faith who has helped many by her charitable acts of giving.

Where should we tithe? Any organization that we are attracted to that serves the greater good is a fine choice. The greater good means for the benefit of all touched and affected by the organization. It also means that people, creatures, the earth or the universe are bettered in some way by the efforts of the organization. Organizations where people are spiritually empowered are good places to tithe because of the "ripple" effect. This is because each person who is empowered will, in turn, empower many others. A single act of kindness, giving or charity can impact many people's lives. We may never know exactly how many people we reach, affect or heal when we give.

When loved ones in spirit deliver messages to clients in sessions, they communicate their gratitude for donations given in their name. They are happy that their legacy lives on in helping others. I have explained to clients that from the loved one's perspective in spirit, one of the most important concerns a soul has is humanitarianism and unconditional love. This is often in sharp contrast to the client's more mundane concerns such as, "Did Aunt Tillie like the people and flowers at her funeral?" or 'Is Dad pleased about the remodeling we did with his inheritance money?" When we make transition, we see the "ripple" effect of our entire life, including how much we gave to others. We are able to see and feel the overall effect our actions have had on others. We are shown in panoramic view how a relatively insignificant act of giving on our part helped to transform someone's life. It is always wonderfully inspiring when a client's loved one comes through in a session and reveals this type of information. This speaks about our need to release expectation and judgment when we give with an open heart.

I recommend that people tithe to an organization or cause to which they feel a deep affinity. For example, if you love animals, give to an organization that works to end animal abuse. When we infuse tithing with the energy of deep feeling, it magnifies the gift many times. There is one note of caution here, however. It is most helpful if we can give our time, money or goods to a cause that is *for* something and not *against* anything or anyone. An example of this may be cited in the recent support by many people of *anti*-terrorism groups and organizations. Any group that carries the label of "anti" cannot hold the purpose to work for the greater good because by its very nature it is opposing something. We would do well to shift our support to a cause that promotes peace and unity among all people. Remember that what holds our focus and energy expands and it is certainly preferable to expand peace instead of terrorism. It is a subtle yet crucial shift in thinking.

A final word about tithing concerns the intent behind it. We give because fundamentally we believe in the infinite resources of the universe. We give from an understanding that what we offer to others, we ultimately give to ourselves and the world. A good affirmation that I use when I tithe is, "I give this gift in the service of the Creator's work through this organization. May it be multiplied many times to benefit the good of all people/animals. Amen." I then bless the gift and release it to the universe. Because I feel so richly blessed, I have learned to release any expectation of return from my giving. However, I have noticed that magically, most of what I have given is almost immediately returned to me in one form or another.

As in other areas of our lives, we are in direct control of the flow of abundance. We can either block it and live in a state of lack or open it to a greater degree and experience the multitude of blessings that the universe offers to us. The choice, as always, is ours.

Questions and Exercises for Self-Enlightenment

1. What is your personal definition of abundance? Be specific in listing everything it means to you. If you could have and be exactly what you wanted in life, what would you have/be? See yourself actively having and being what you listed. How does it feel?

2. In your journal, list several painful situations you've experienced. Looking back, how are these blessings? How have you grown as a result of having experienced them? Ask God to help you begin to forgive others who have hurt you. Open your heart to receive the flow of gratitude for these situations.

3. Take inventory of your tribal beliefs about prosperity. Did you come from a family that always thought there was never enough to go around? From one that believed you must struggle to get ahead in life? How have you internalized these beliefs? How have they affected your life? How can you change them?

4. When you think back over your life, what has given you the greatest joy? The most pain? How have these been related to how you view prosperity in your life? In what ways do you feel blocked from opening to prosperity?

5. Tithe to an organization of your choice today and bless it.

11

SPIRIT CONSCIOUSNESS: ANGELS, HEALERS, TEACHERS AND OTHER SPIRIT GUIDES

One evening in meditation, an old man with a long, billowy beard that reached to the floor greeted me. His beard was so long in my mind's eye that it seemed to be endless, filling my entire vision with its soft whiteness. As I watched him approach me in the garden I was sitting in, I felt a great sense of peace and protection. He sauntered up to me and rested his cane on the ground beside me. When I looked into his eyes, I felt the centuries, perhaps millenniums, of wisdom behind them. He communicated to me without opening his mouth: "My name is Lazarus. I am with you to help you understand and love yourself more fully. Call upon me whenever you want wise counsel." I felt as if I was talking to my grandfather, yet I had no conscious memory of ever meeting this man before. His compassion and sincerity shined forth from his aura. His wisdom was incomparable to anyone I had ever met. The unconditional love I felt in his presence was gently reassuring. I have seen him many times since then, and each time I am in awe of his presence.

He comes to me when I am in need of spiritual guidance or in some sort of transition. I call him the "spiritual alchemist."

-From one of my own meditations

Who are the spirit guides* who assist us on our journey throughout life and how are we connected to them? How can they help us live our lives from a more loving perspective? How do we link up with them? Have we known them in past lives? This chapter is about the relationships we form and maintain with our spiritual companions before we come to earth and while we are here. Incidentally, since we are primarily concerned with our lives here and now in the physical realm, we will confine our discussion to this dimension—although our advisors help us in all phases of our growth, including time spent without physical form. They may be with us through many incarnations to continue the development and fulfillment of our soul's expression and purpose.

As previously explained, when we decide to take physical form and leave our dwelling in the world of spirit, we review our soul's experiences and the karmic responsibilities that still need to be balanced and healed. Based upon this assessment of our growth, we consult with our spiritual advisors to formulate a plan for our imminent incarnation. Our advisors help us take stock of our soul's deepest needs and the challenges we must confront in order to fulfill them— as well as the earthly circumstances that will most effectively enable us to do so. In essence, they help us plan our lives. They are qualified to help us because they are very familiar with us on a soul level, and have known us from past incarnations. Frequently, they are a member of the same soul group as we are, which means they share a similarity of purpose.

Who They Are—The Mirror

Each of our spiritual companions is a reflection of some aspect of us; actually they are not distinct from us. How can this be? In the mind of God there is no separation. All is one and one is all. This applies to the entire universe, including our relationships with our advisors. Because there is no separation (only our perception of it), we are always united with our guides on a soul level. There is constant communication between us because we are actually communicating with ourselves. Sound confusing? Think of a mirror. The reflection we see when we stand in front of it is ours, even though it appears to be physically separate from us. It is still us; the reflection is simply an outward projection. The same is true of our advisors; they are an outward projection of our soul essence. Just as we are one with our brothers and sisters of earth, we are one with our spiritual companions.

Based on our reason for coming to the earth's schoolroom, we attract corresponding "specialty" advisors who assist us on our life's pathway. Take, for example, a soul who needs to express and balance karma concerning the qualities of nurturing and compassion. One of the ways he may choose to do so is by entering the medical field. He would then have advisors who would assist in this particular vocation

At the same time they are assisting us, our advisors are meeting and balancing their own karma, unless they are one of the Ascended Masters (who have met and balanced all karma) or angels (who have never been in physical form and are therefore not subject to karma). Our guides learn from us, just as we do from them. By helping us, they also learn and grow. This mutual relationship with our guides is always

---

* The words "guides," "advisors," and "companions" may be interchanged, as they all refer to the same beings.

a cooperative effort. Much like our earthly families, our guides choose us and we choose them for maximum spiritual growth in any given lifetime.

Let's take the above example of the soul who chooses to balance karma by entering into a vocation such as medicine. (Incidentally, the past experiences of the soul also influence direction and purpose for future lifetimes. In this instance, this soul may have been a healer in one or many lifetimes and is best able to use these abilities to uplift humanity and at the same time meet karmic responsibilities.) The spiritual advisors who will assist this soul may be healers and spirit doctors who channel healing energies to earth. Spirit doctors are those who were once doctors while in physical form and are currently choosing to help souls on similar pathways. If the individual happens to be involved in the field of medical research, his advisors may be spirit scientists who work from the higher dimensions to channel information to him concerning important ideas and innovations for the advancement and betterment of humanity. According to divine timing and plan, the information is channeled to earth when human consciousness is at the proper level of receptivity for these new ideas.

Soul Groups

A soul group is one in which similar vibration and purpose unites all within it. There are millions of soul groups that exist in all dimensions, yet all are joined by the unity of God. Each exists for the purpose of spiritual advancement of its members, collective humanity and the greater harmony of the universe. You have undoubtedly had the experience of resonating with another person at a deep emotional or spiritual level. Chances are the two of you are from the same soul group. Because our advisors are usually members of our soul group, they are able to connect with us at the very deepest level, sharing all of our experiences. They are aware of our karmic lessons and probable pathways when we are born, and they have agreed to assist us in any way possible. However, no guide, teacher, healer or angel can ever supersede our gift of free will, which is our birthright. We always have the ability to change our minds and redirect the course of our lives through choice and will. Our advisors offer counsel and direction regardless of the pathways we choose in life. They love us unconditionally and always respect our right to exert our free will in whatever manner we wish.

There are many different groups of advisors who assist us in the journey of life. I have included the most common ones who help us. Please note that there are other groups that also exist in addition to the ones listed. Additionally, it is important to keep in mind that no advisor can ever disregard our free will. Their role is to inspire, guide and assist us in fulfilling our life's purpose. Our guides cannot and will not do our work for us, although they are with us every step of the way.

Loved Ones

Loved ones who have passed into the world of spirit can and do act as guides for us. They do not necessarily fill the same role as the other spirit advisors in assisting us in fulfilling life purpose, but nonetheless may inspire, protect and guide us in the best way they can. The bond of love that exists with our loved ones allows the connection to remain intact long after their passing. They can feel and hear our thoughts and emotions from the spirit world, and regularly send us love, prayer and healing energy. We can strengthen the connection by returning these gifts of love to them. This is especially important immediately after their passing. Prayers of love and healing help to uplift them and heal us from feelings of grief that keep us from moving on with life.

Today, an increasing number of people desire to know more about what happens when we make transition to the world of spirit. People want to develop the ability to receive and send messages of love, guidance and reassurance to those in spirit. The truth is, we all have the ability to do so if we desire. We merely need to raise our awareness to a level of acceptance that communication is possible, and then remain open to engage in it. When clients come for readings in which loved ones communicate, I encourage them to continue the communication after the session. A good way to do this is to simply send love to those in spirit and *ask* them to communicate with you. Most are happy to oblige.

Much like our other spiritual guides, our loved ones speak to us in many different ways and through various channels. Gently impressing us with their thoughts and feelings is one way they let us know of their presence. One of the most common questions I hear from clients is, "How do I tell the difference between my thoughts and those of my loved ones?" (This question can also apply to the communication we receive from our other spiritual advisors and is one that involves the ability to use discernment.) The answer to this question is, ironically, another question: How does the information received from the communication make you feel? When we are receiving messages from our loved ones and spirit guides, we will feel uplifted, loved and guided. When it is our own thoughts and feelings we are sensing, the messages may be more reflective of our personal issues—including our doubts, insecurities and fears. It is important to keep in mind that spirit advisors always work with and through our soul, for our highest and best good. Our loved ones are no exception in that they remain connected to us through the bond of love.

Another common way in which loved ones may reach us is through the impression of a scent that was associated with them. Often, the spirit will impress the thought of the scent, such as a favorite perfume or cologne, upon our thoughts.

Our sense of smell is closely connected to our memories of people, places and things, and may evoke these memories in us quite readily. Our loved ones are aware of this and use it to let us know they are near. Some people have also reported smelling a particular flower, such as a rose, which may carry special meaning to them. Sometimes our loved ones will impress upon us the smell of medication they were taking before passing. I have had this phenomenon occur in readings when the spirit comes back into the earth vibration with memories. When a spirit who smoked is communicating, I will smell the tobacco. Pets that come from the spirit world also communicate their presence with the use of scent. I remember one phone session in which the communicating spirit's smelly dog made an appearance!

As a medium, I have witnessed how ingenious some spirits can be when they want to get their message across to a loved one on earth. I have known them to use the telephone, lights, and the television to communicate their presence. I once did a reading for Anna, whose husband communicated in the session that he planned on leaving a "voice" message on her answering machine. Sure enough, the next time I saw Anna, she told me that two days after the reading, she received a strange message on her answering machine from a barely audible voice. Since she had never heard any message like this before, she was certain it was from Tom, her deceased husband.

Loved ones may move items in someone's home, office or car to attract attention. Often this is done to attract the attention of others to think of them or pay attention to particular circumstances—such as a warning of danger, or meaningful events that coincide with the time. It is common for loved ones to send us signals around or on their birthday, anniversary, or date of passing. The communication is enhanced because it's more likely that we are thinking about them at these times. Sometimes they may even impress us to tune into a certain song on the radio that happened to be their favorite, or that communicates a special message that we need to hear in times of trouble.

Messages From Beyond

Why do our loved ones come to us after their passing? Above all else, they want us to be aware of their continued existence in the world of spirit. Some of the communication they send to us can simply be summed up as, "Hey! I'm alive! Don't talk about me as if I'm dead. I'm as real and alive as you are and life here is great!" I have experienced spirits' communication of gratitude for something that was done after their passing. In a session with a young woman who had a friend in spirit, the spirit friend expressed her gratitude for an endowment fund that had been given in her name by friends and family. The fund was to help people with the same illness as hers. During another session with a woman who had planted trees in her deceased husband's honor, he sent acknowledgment and thanks for this kind remembrance.

Another reason loved ones in spirit communicate with us is to offer reassurance during difficult times. They want us to know they are still aware of our earthly challenges and are able to send love, prayer and healing that can make a difference in our lives. In this way, they act as guides in our spiritual growth because they are able to see the "big picture" from the spirit world. Often the communicating spirit will impart messages concerning the importance of love and forgiveness. Even if a person is not the kindest or friendliest on earth, he or she has the chance to heal in the world of spirit and communicate newfound perspective. In many respects, these souls can give us the most powerful insights into our own situations and challenges. They can help us to understand priorities in life and the consequences of our thoughts, feelings and actions. They inspire us to learn from their experiences and possibly avoid the pain they went through in their earthly lives.

Perhaps our loved ones' most intriguing messages have to do with the nature of the afterlife. In many readings, they share experiences and knowledge about the world of spirit. An example of this can be found in a session with Rita, whose husband communicated with her regularly about what happens when we pass over. I suggested to her that she record these insights in writing because it was apparent that they had a contract between them for this exchange of information. Rita revealed that she had always been fascinated by the afterlife and wanted to know what it is like when we pass. Interestingly, when her husband was alive, he didn't believe in the afterlife. During one communication, he shared his experience of traveling through a tunnel of light after leaving his body. He also told her he changed his beliefs concerning the survival of the soul after physical death. Rita said she had noticed that since her husband's passing, she was distinctly aware of his presence on many occasions. This communication was healing for both Rita and her husband, allowing them to continue their relationship beyond the physical realm.

Another fascinating session involved Lora, whose husband, Frank, came through very clearly with thoughts and images about one way communication happens from the spirit world. Lora comes for a reading every year around the anniversary of Frank's passing. During the session, Frank showed me an image of a portal through which those in spirit can see and communicate with their loved ones on earth. It resembled the type of telescope commonly found in tourist areas on scenic overlooks. He said he had to put his request in to the "gatekeepers," who help monitor the portal, so he could communicate with Lora. "I know how important this is to you so I put my request in to be here for you today," he said. "There were many ahead of me waiting to come through to their loved ones." He showed me a long line of souls waiting to come through the portal so they could talk to their loved ones on earth. To let Lora know he still watched over her and the family, Frank communicated messages about their two children. "Jason needs more help with math," he said. "Look into getting a tutor. I was so proud of Amber when she danced in the school production last month." Throughout the session, I was struck with the clarity and depth of Frank's thoughts. I could tell he had spent some time studying and practicing the art of communication from the spirit world after his passing.

Communication is a two-way street. We must raise our sensitivity to be able to clearly communicate with souls in the spirit world; those who have crossed over must lower their thoughts to be able to communicate with those on earth. A gatekeeper in the spirit world assists in this process by acting as a "bridge" between the two. Mediums have several gatekeepers who facilitate communication to and from the spirit world. They are translators who help to focus and clarify the thoughts of communicating spirits.

Not all loved ones communicate as clearly as Frank. It takes practice, focus and determination. Because we retain our personality traits, if we don't communicate clearly when we're on earth, we won't do it after passing. We go through a training process to learn how to lower our thoughts to "speak" with mediums and our loved ones on earth. The success of many sessions depends on both the skill of the communicating spirit and the medium's interpretation of the information.

A common vehicle for spirit communication is the dream state. When we sleep, our conscious mind rests and the subconscious becomes extremely active. We travel from earth's third dimensional consciousness to the fourth dimension where our loved ones commonly reside. Some clients have related dreams in which they're in close contact with their relatives, feeling as if they were actually with them. A common facet of such dreams seems to be their clarity and vividness. The emotions that accompany the dream are love, forgiveness or reassurance. Sometimes the departed spirit appears to tell the dreamer he is safe, alive and out of pain in the spirit world. This is particularly true when the dream happens immediately after the person's passing. People who report having these contacts usually relate their feelings of relief upon knowing their family member is indeed alive and well after crossing over.

When to Call Upon a Loved One

It is generally not necessary to call upon loved ones; the bond of love naturally connects them to us. Our loved ones sense our thoughts and emotions. In many instances, they attempt to facilitate healing and forgiveness. To strengthen the connection, send love and ask them to come to you when both of you are ready. Remember that each soul has the right to do as he or she wishes and may not always desire to visit with us. If you don't hear from someone, it doesn't mean that he or she doesn't love you. If the communication won't benefit both of you in some way, it won't take place.

You may also use a photograph (which captures a person's life-force energy on film) of your loved one to connect more strongly. Send love to the person in the photo as you look at it to strengthen the bond.

Angels

The angelic kingdom has influenced us to the extent that many books have been written on it. There are thousands of angels that can and do assist humankind in many different and wonderful ways. Each comes with a particular quality of the Creator's mind or energy and they bring these to us in a loving, gentle manner. The inspiration they bring is sometimes so subtle that we may not receive the message if our minds are not open to it. Angels carry a sincere intent to respect our free will. They want to be of service, and never wish to frighten us. Angelic messages are like a breath of spring air on a clear, sunny day. They are *always* in accordance with divine will and grace.

The angels have many means through which they can deliver messages: gentle thoughts that slip into our minds, music, poetry, nature, and other people. Like all of our guides, they come to us through the path of least resistance. They always speak to us in ways that we are most likely to understand. From the beginning of time and to present day, they are messengers of God and have a singularity of purpose: the desire to assist us in our soul's growth. The angels can be our intimate companions, understanding our personalities, weaknesses and deepest fears without our saying a word.

Some angelic qualities are beauty, faith, communication, freedom, communication, knowledge, manifestation and gratitude, among others. When we wish to draw a specific quality to us, we can call on the angel who carries this quality. They are always ready to assist us in whatever way possible, but we must indicate our willingness for their help by asking.

Each of us has a guardian angel assigned to us before birth and who stays with us throughout our lifetime. In fact, this special angel may stay with us throughout many incarnations for purposes of our spiritual development. The angel's main purposes are guardianship (over our physical safety, especially when we are infants or in a vulnerable state at any point in our lives) and inspiration to follow our soul's pathway. In matters of physical safety, they lovingly protect us and gently remove us from harm's way, as long as it is not part of our karmic contract to experience such an occurrence. Stories abound of miraculous angelic interventions in dangerous and deadly situations in people's lives. This brings up an important characteristic of the angels: the ability to take on physical form when necessary. Because their vibration is so high, they are able to do many things that we would consider impossible. There are stories of angels who have rescued people from drowning, falling, crashing their car and other life-threatening circumstances. As messengers of God, the angels have special power to do what is necessary to help us in any way. They are dedicated, in all respects, to the utmost good of humanity. They may intervene in disastrous and catastrophic events, such as the collapse of a building, a war, or a national emergency. We all know someone who has been "touched by an angel." A client once shared with me that she believed an angel had prevented her baby daughter from choking to death. Another credited her angel for protecting her through many years of domestic abuse.

Our guardian angels, along with countless others from the angelic kingdom, constantly surround us and impress us with uplifting and empowering thoughts of inspiration to help us overcome thinking that is not in accordance with God. Their gentle yet powerful assurance envelops us in unconditional love.

The following is a partial list of some of the angels and the particular qualities each brings to the ministry of humankind. For a more complete listing, along with a detailed explanation of each, see *Angel Blessings, Cards of Sacred Guidance & Inspiration* by Kimberly Marooney (Merrill-West Publishing, 1995.)

Archangel Gabriel—resurrection.
Archangel Raphael—healing.
Ramaela—joy.
Israfel—music.
Shushienae—purity.
Soqued Hozi—partnership.
Raziel—knowledge.
Iofiel—beauty.
Zagzagel—wisdom.
Nathaniel—fire.
Charmiene—harmony.

Archangel Michael—protection.
Archangel Uriel—ministration.
Mihr—relationships.
Metatron—thought.
Hadraniel—love.
Ooniemme—gratitude.
Ongkanon—communication.
Amitiel—truth.
Shekinah—unity.
Micah—divine plan.
Uzziel—faith.

Times You May Want to Call Upon the Angels

You may call upon the angels whenever you wish; they are always available to assist you in every possible way. However, you may want to ask for specific guidance and inspiration concerning a certain task, relationship or situation that seems to have exhausted your capabilities of understanding. In these cases, ask for the angel who embodies the particular quality or assistance you need to help you. Remember to release your expectation of how the answer will come. You may also wish to call upon the angels for protection while traveling, when you are ill or when you are faced with a difficult challenge.

Spiritual Teachers

Teachers agree to assist and instruct us with a specific career, task, project or assignment that we have contracted to do. I call these teachers "specialty guides" because they come with a specific type of knowledge necessary for the completion of tasks related to our soul purpose. For example, if we have agreed to perform counseling as part of our purpose, a counseling teacher is "assigned" who will help us.

Teachers may connect with us before birth or at any point in our lives. They may remain with us for years or just a few months. They may work with us intensely, giving us mountains of information, or they may assist us from the sidelines, simply reassuring us that we're doing a good job. They can act as overseers of special projects we take on— such as coordinating a volunteer organization—impressing us with valuable information that comes from our intuition. Because they are not limited by a physical perspective, they are able to help us see the larger picture of what is needed in a given situation.

A teaching guide is one who is deemed qualified to assist

us by a Board of Advisors in the spirit world. This board is comprised of superior teaching guides who are in charge of an examination process necessary for the qualification to help others. Spirit teachers undergo rigorous examinations by working with many different souls in their specific area of expertise. This is usually done as an apprenticeship, during which the aspiring teacher works with a more experienced one who has already "graduated." The phenomenon of apprenticeship is quite common in the world of spirit, much like in the physical world. One cannot advance from novice to master without proper training, and the spirit world is no exception. Upon completion of the necessary training, teachers become available to those who are in need of their knowledge.

Some examples of specific areas that may herald the arrival of or connection to a teacher are: technological inventions that require certain facts and information, medical research, counseling, politics, spiritual disciplines and teaching. An example of a specialized field that requires a spirit teacher is computer technology. Interestingly, some clients who have come for readings from this profession have teachers with knowledge of crystals and energetic grid patterns that seem to be connected with the ancient civilization of Atlantis. This seems to be particularly true of people who were born in the 1980's. The specialty advisors of these individuals are able to assist in the development of current technology by channeling this ancient wisdom so it can be implemented today.

All of humankind's advanced ideas, research, and technologies have been realized as a result of the invaluable assistance from the spirit realms. Although they are generally unaware of it, individuals who work in technological fields act as channels for many advancements with the cooperation of spirit teachers.

When to Call on a Teacher

Depending on our life mission, we attract to us an appropriate teacher who has the knowledge we require. Just because we are not aware of the teacher does not mean he or she doesn't exist. Call upon your teacher whenever you need special guidance related to your specific field of endeavor. Many teachers communicate with us in the dream state because it is the time we are the most receptive. Record your dreams and any pertinent information that comes through. Most importantly, ask to receive the guidance or information you are requesting in an easily understandable form. Our teachers adjust to meet our requirements to understand their messages. Remember to be specific. Record in writing what is revealed to you.

Healers

There are souls in the spirit world whose main purpose is to channel healing energies to the physical world. These are healers who assist humankind in many and varied ways whenever they are called upon. This group includes, but is not limited to, some of the angels (Raphael particularly), spirit doctors and nurses (who may also be considered teachers), fifth dimensional light beings and certain groups of extraterrestrial beings. In some cases, these souls are continuing the work they started while in body (because our soul's growth never ceases, we may choose to carry on a particular pathway from the spirit world.)

As a spiritual healer, I have been assisted by many wonderful souls in spirit who work with me to channel healing energies. Two of these are a spirit doctor who once worked on the battlefields in World War II and a pathologist who lived and practiced during the 20th century. Each assists me in sensing the etheric (the energy field just above the physical in vibration) body of those who come for healing. Since spirit doctors have the ability to see energy fields, they can act as guides for a healer. They do this by gently impressing thoughts upon the healer where an imbalance exists and the correct placement of the healer's hands to channel energy into the proper area.

Healers in spirit most likely assist any person who has a life mission of helping others. However, this is not the only manner in which healing guides come in. In times of catastrophe, disaster, war or illness, healers are busily working from the spirit world to lend assistance. They may work beside the angels in times of need. Because they are dedicated to the mission of helping to ease humankind's suffering, the healers work tirelessly to aid anyone who is suffering— including the sick and injured, medical doctors and surgeons, and those in mental distress. There are even healers for the animal and plant kingdoms!

Souls who were once members of the clergy while on earth are often found in the healers' group. A former Catholic nun whom I have often sensed and once encountered in my sleep assists one of my colleagues who is a spiritual healer. A beautifully gentle soul, she unselfishly channels love and healing whenever the opportunity presents itself. In addition to the clergy, a large number of souls who were once Native Americans seem to be plentiful among the healers. This is perhaps due to the fact that the Natives maintained a strong and reverent regard for the earth and natural healing methods. I have met many healers and herbalists who sense that they are being assisted by Native guides and healers. I have clairvoyantly seen some of them standing behind these individuals. During a hands-on healing session, the spirit healers may place their etheric hands (hands made up of energy and thought) overtop of the healer's hands. This condenses the healing energy and brings it down to the physical plane to be used more effectively.

Like all guides, healers cannot violate our free will or karmic lessons, even in times of trouble. But they can and do help us wherever and whenever they can in accordance with divine plan and will.

When to Call on a Healer

Do not hesitate to call upon a healer when you are sick or in need of healing. The best way to summon them is to ask for a soul who brings light, love and healing energy to come "now." It is important to say the word 'now" because the spirit world has no concept of time, but they do feel the immediacy of "now." When the healer works with you, you may be impressed to do certain things such as eat particular foods (for their healing nutrients), take certain supplements, (to help change the vibratory frequency of the body) or drink more fluids (to flush out toxic build-up.) The healers often work with us at night when we are the most receptive to receiving energy. They work with the natural energetic flow of the body at all times. If you are impressed to do something differently in your daily routine, it is probably needed for balance or repair of the body.

Joy Guides

Joy guides remind us of the lighter nature of our soul. They assist us in maintaining balance and levity in the midst of life challenges we face. A natural extension of our innate joy, these guides inspire us in a playful, gentle and sometimes humorous manner.

Have you ever awakened in the morning with a song playing in your head that just won't go away? This is one way the joy guides will impress us with the messages we need to hear. They may also come to us by pointing out the overlooked humor in an otherwise serious situation. At times, they are the purveyors of jokes that come to us through the written or spoken word of others. They may appear to us in our dreams as clowns, jesters, or in some other non-threatening way to let us know they are with us. I have clairvoyantly seen them appear as comic book heroes or popular television characters. Do you remember Tony the Tiger from the Frosted Flakes commercials? When I first began meditating, he frolicked into view with a smile. After our initial meeting, he began to appear in my meditations roaring, "It's greaaaaaat!" when I celebrated accomplishments in my life. He reminds me to lighten up and not take life so seriously. Whenever he visits me, I feel the joy, laughter, and fun of my childhood again.

Although joy guides are essentially light-hearted in their demeanor, they nonetheless serve an equally important and valuable function as our other guides. They remind us of the necessity of balance in our lives. They may come to us when we are having a "down" day or when we feel burdened by the responsibilities of life. We have all heard the expression, "laughter is the best medicine" and in this respect, joy guides are true healers. Periodically we need to experience the healing effects of a genuine smile and a hearty laugh. Sometimes we need to just play. This is the domain of the joy guides.

One of my joy guides is Rolf. I first met him three years ago in the middle of a healing I received. He initially appeared to me as a caterpillar with tennis shoes on every foot! I then heard his name clearly in my head. Since that day, I have had many encounters with Rolf and he has communicated many messages to me. Appearing in Austrian attire of short, green trousers with suspenders, he has chosen to maintain the identity of his last incarnation during the mid 20th century. Sometimes I see him in an area of the spirit world with mountains and snow. I can't tell you the number of times I have heard and seen him singing, dancing and yodeling. He has shared with me how humor became such a necessary element of his life during World War II when his family was torn apart by the devastation of the war. Sometimes humor was the only thing that pulled him through the horror of war. He developed a knack for it and chose to continue using his gift from the spirit world. The day after Rolf shared this information, I read a book that said the very same thing: in deeply troubling times, people turn to humor, song and dance to alleviate tension. I knew this was a confirmation of what he had told me.

Joy guides are spirit friends who enable us to see life from a different perspective. In the direst of circumstances they remind us to view a situation with optimism. In other instances such as teaching or speaking, these guides help us to more effectively communicate a complex or tedious concept by the interjection of humor. They do this by inspiring us with creative or humorous ideas to balance our presentation.

When to Call on Joy Guides

Call on these guides whenever a situation calls for light-heartedness or laughter. You may also want to connect more strongly with joy guides when you are feeling down or stuck in a rut. If speaking or teaching is a part of your career, you may wish to ask for special inspiration from these guides. The next time you hear a song in your head, pay close attention to the lyrics to see what message your guides are communicating to you.

Nature Spirits

Nature spirits communicate with plants, flowers, trees, insects, and the earth. Their primary purpose is to help sustain life in all forms. They uplift humankind and the planet by supporting and nourishing their growth. The nature spirits may take many forms, depending on the particular life form they are connected to. Some give and receive life-force energy specifically from plants. Others live in the earth's great bodies of water. Gemstones, minerals, and rocks also contain nature spirits within them.

Most nature spirits have never been in human form, yet have been intricately connected with human consciousness for centuries. Celtic and Greek legends and mythologies make frequent references to the presence of friendly fairy and nature spirits that interact and play with humans in clever and magical ways. Stories of elves, wood nymphs, dancing water spirits, and fairy folk have made their way into the cultural legends of many countries, especially European ones. The leprechaun, a type of elf who possesses hidden treasure, is one such example from Irish folklore. Another example is the troll, a creature who purportedly lives under bridges or in caves, according to Scandinavian legends.

The fairy is a nature spirit that has been particularly associated with tales and legends of England. In many of these, fairies often transport humans into mystical, magical realms beyond earthly existence. These are the realms of imagination where anything is possible, and the ethereal world of dreams beyond our conscious awareness. The message of the fairies is one that captures the innocence, wonder and playfulness of childhood. These wonderful beings remind us to let go of the limitations we place on what is real and possible in our lives. They inspire us to open our awareness to other states of being—and above all else, to play. The story of Peter Pan and Tinkerbell—who taught children to fly and release their fear—is a good example of the magical role nature spirits and fairies can play in our lives. Release of our limitations and expectations can transport us to new and exciting realms of existence and thought.

Although folklore depicts nature spirits in human form, they can assume any form they desire. If you are observant, you may sense them in the trees, plants, streams, and mountains of the earth. You may see their faces in a piece of driftwood or on the petal of a beautiful flower. These spirits sometimes act as companions to wildlife and therefore are closely associated with animals, birds and insects. They sustain the current of life-force energy by nourishing Mother Earth.

When to Call on Nature Spirits

If you work with the earth (such as farming or gardening) call upon nature spirits to help you. They bring life supporting energy to all living things. If you work with herbal remedies and/or flower essences for healing, nature spirits can assist you in maintaining the purity of the plant's essence. They may also supply you with information regarding the optimal healing use of each plant. Call on them in meditation or anytime you wish to connect deeply with nature and the earth.

Animal Guides

Another group of guides that come to assist us are from the world of spirit animals, which is as rich and diverse as the human spirit world. Each animal and bird on earth also exists in spirit form and can act as a companion guide to us, depending on the specific qualities that are needed for our soul's growth. The lion, for example, embodies the qualities of courage, strength and leadership. The eagle comes with the attributes of valor, swiftness and transcendence. Every member of the bird and animal kingdom resonates with specific characteristics that make it unique and powerful in its own right. They come to express these qualities and experience life in the physical world just as we do.

The spirituality, legends and stories of Native Americans contain numerous references to the wisdom of the bird and animal kingdoms and their interconnectedness with humans. Because of the Natives' deep reverence and attunement to the earth, sky, and cosmos, they feel connected to all lifeforms. Plants, trees, animals, insects and water are believed to embody and radiate the love, harmony, and wisdom of Great Spirit, the Creator. Shamans, the tribal medicine people, frequently call upon animal guides to assist them in ritual healings and ceremonies. Animal skin, fur and feathers are often used to link an individual with the characteristics and wisdom of a certain animal species. Central to this culture's belief systems is the idea that man is one with everything, and thus looks to nature for knowledge and reflection of himself. Many modern-day spiritual seekers embrace Native beliefs of the interconnectedness and unity of all of life.

We can call upon a particular animal to come to us when we need its special attribute. Some examples: dog—loyalty and companionship; cat—absorption of negative energy and enhancement of psychic ability; wolf—guardianship and vigilance; turtle—patience and endurance; elephant—physical strength and wisdom; swan—spiritual transformation and beauty; rabbit—fertility, rebirth and swiftness. For further examples and more complete listings, an excellent reference book is Ted Andrews' *Animal Speak (Llewellyn Publications, 1993)*.

Occasionally, we may sense an animal guide's spirit around us. They communicate their presence by leaving a feather in our pathway, impressing us to buy an image of them, or making an appearance in our dreams. They appreciate when we recognize them in any way. Sometimes we might see or come in contact with the physical form of the spirit animal. This happened to me shortly after a friend did a reading for me in which the mouse appeared as one of my animal teachers. For quite a while after, my house seemed to be invaded by them! I did not kill them, as I knew they had come not only for food, but to teach me about the qualities of inquisitiveness and invention.

When to Call on Animal Guides

When in need of a certain quality or particular strength of character, call upon the animal or bird that is representative of it. Find photos of the animal with which you wish to associate and put them in a place where you will see them frequently. If you are involved in the caretaking of animals in any way, call upon the animal spirits to help you communicate with and care for your animals. Physical animals have guides just as humans do and they act in much the same way. In this respect, don't hesitate to call upon the animal healers for pets that are sick or injured.

Guides are part of our spiritual family that love us unconditionally. Do not think of them as superior to you in any way and don't hesitate to call upon them when you need a universal point of view for a concern you have. Allow them to gently impress you with the guidance you are seeking.

A final word needs to be said concerning the names of our spiritual companions. Many times, guides will not introduce themselves by name because they have spent an equivalent of many earthly years in the spirit world where they are recognized by the quality of their vibration, as opposed to a finite syllable such as a name. This applies to most of the highly evolved guides. Sometimes, however, our guides *will* impress us with a name for *our* purposes of identification of them. Do not feel as if you are not connected to your guides if you don't receive a name from them; you will recognize them by their love.

Questions and Exercises for Self-Enlightenment

1. In your journal, review your answers to previous questions regarding your life's purpose. What types of guides are likely connected to you in fulfilling your purpose? Would they be teachers, healers or nature spirits? In what ways have you sensed their presence?

2. Sometimes, we are aware of our guides at a young age. What are your childhood experiences involving "imaginary" playmates? Do you remember seeing and believing in fairies? How did you feel about these beings? How did they help you?

3. Is there a loved one in spirit with whom you wish to reconnect? Try this: Hold a photo of the person in your hand for several minutes while you remember loving qualities associated with this person. Recall fond memories of time spent together. Repeat his or her name several times as you continue to send love. Now just sit and be receptive to your feelings. What are you sensing? Allow your loved one to speak to you. Visualize the two of you having a conversation. What is being communicated? Write your experiences.

4. Think of animals you like or are drawn to. What qualities are they bringing to you? To reinforce their presence in your life, keep drawings, photos or plush toys of these animals in your home. Is there a certain animal that continually reappears in your life? Based on its qualities, what message is it bringing to you?

5. Before going to sleep, ask for one of your guides to come to you during the night. As you drift off to sleep, visualize yourself floating safely in a column of white light in which you drift higher and higher into a beautiful garden. In the morning, take a moment to record your dreams. Did your guide appear? What did he or she look like? Did you receive a message? Record your experiences.

12

BOUND BY CHOICE:
HOW TO MEET AND CONSULT
WITH YOUR SPIRIT GUIDES

M any people ask me, "How do I connect more strongly to my guides and angels? I know they're there, but I can't hear, feel or see them. Can you teach me how to do that?" After I assure them that their guides are in constant contact with them and that the only separation that exists is in their own minds, they often persist in believing that they have somehow been disconnected from their spiritual advisors. This is due to the fact that in the physical plane, we live with the illusion of being separate from other worlds of spirit. In reality, we are one with all of creation, including higher planes of consciousness. Although it is difficult for us to conceive of it, we exist on many levels of consciousness at the same time. The physical plane is only one of many.

When we start to awaken in a spiritual sense, we begin to have vague memories of our ancestry in the spirit worlds. We experience feelings of discontent and start asking questions that lead us on a quest to find meaning in our lives: I am highly successful in my career—why doesn't that fulfill me? Who am I apart from my marriage? Why do I feel so directionless and lonely? Is *this* all there is to life? Tired of the emptiness of what the ego and personality tell us *should* be enough, we begin to search deeply within ourselves to connect with the core essence of our soul. In this search, one that is only possible by going within, we begin to regain a sense of wholeness in rediscovering our true spiritual identities.

In the process of going within, we reawaken unconscious memories of the spiritual companions who have agreed to assist us on our journey through the physical world. This is the point at which many people begin to become aware of the connection with their guides. As children, we may easily see, talk to and play with our spiritual companions. As we mature, we block our perception of them, in order to fit in with society and our peers. Years later, we may rekindle these experiences and memories during meditation. Some people become aware of their guides during dreams in which they remember spending time with others who are familiar, yet unidentifiable. One of my guides came to me in this manner. One night, when I was just starting to fall asleep, I sensed a beautiful young woman with long black hair and a dark complexion walking beside me on a country road. She wore a jewel in the center of her forehead and clothing that looked as if it was from Persia. Her presence startled me so much that I immediately woke up. Later, I received "proof" of her existence when I bought a piece of channeled artwork that depicted the psychic artist's interpretation of my spirit guides and teachers. In the foreground of the drawing, was a young woman with long, dark hair, holding a crescent—a symbol that dates back to ancient Byzantine times. I recognized the woman in the painting as the same one who visited me in my dream. Since this first meeting, I have come to realize that she helps me to embrace the qualities of feminine beauty and grace.

Opening our intuitive senses is much like waking up on a brilliantly sunny summer day after sleeping through a long, bleak winter. Our spiritual companions celebrate each and every awakening we have, no matter how minor of a breakthrough we think it is. They laugh with us, they flood us with compassion when we stumble during the process of spiritual growth and they gently impress us with the remembrance of our spiritual identities. Like any relationship, the one with our guides requires our attention and support if it is to become stronger. The more we put into it, the more we'll receive. How do we go about strengthening the connection with our guides?

The Importance of Discernment

Discernment is extremely important when one is beginning to connect with spiritual guidance. While guides are usually of the highest intent and purpose, it is possible to connect with entities that are manipulative and sometimes detrimental to our growth. Although this is rarely the case, it is wise to always employ discernment in determining who and what we are connecting to. This is done by clarifying our intent through simple methods of energetic purification. Some of these methods are smudging (burning sage and swirling the smoke in our immediate environment and around our auric field), gemstone protection (black tourmaline is excellent), and simple visualizations (seeing oneself completely surrounded in white light). Affirmations of our intent to connect with only those who come in light and love for our highest good are also helpful. It is through our intent that we originally connect with our guides and they are aware of our energy at all times. When we feel their presence, we are merely shifting our attention to something that has always been a part of us.

A word needs to be said about the importance of understanding that your guides, angels and teachers are not superior to you in any way. Do not make the mistake of believing they are somehow better or more "enlightened" than you. They are merely on a different plane of existence than you are in the present moment. The relationship that we have with our spiritual companions is mutual; both parties learn and grow spiritually through the exchange. Our guides and angels will never deny us help, as long as we ask. I have found it helpful to think of the relationship with my guides as a team in which every player has an equally significant position to play. The roles may be different, but one is not better or preferable to another.

Gateways to Opening and Feeling the Connection With Your Guides

After we have put forth our intent to connect at a deeper level with our guides, how do we do it? The practice of regular meditation is the easiest way to initiate and sustain contact with our spiritual helpers. Meditation enables us to stay in direct contact with messages, symbols and guidance that are constantly being directed our way. A simple form of meditation is the best. Many people believe that they need to practice complicated forms of esoteric meditation in specific postures to be able to connect with higher spiritual dimensions. This is not so. All we need do is to listen in a focused way for short periods of time to gain understanding. If you are just beginning, it is best to meditate for only five or ten minutes so your attention does not have as much opportunity to drift. It is important to choose a regular time of day to still your mind; you will then become accustomed to doing so at that specific time. It is also a good idea to use the same uncluttered, quiet room or space in your home. Each time you enter this room or space, you will subconsciously begin to relax.

Through the practice of meditation, we still our mental "chatter" and open the gateway to intuition. Meditation enhances our innate capacity to feel and experience sensations that lie beyond our physical senses. This is the level where we connect with our guides.

Meditative Journaling

Meditative journaling is one of the most helpful methods to establish and maintain connection with guides. This is a relatively simple process and can be invaluable in understanding ourselves during spiritual growth.

Purchase a journal that will be used *solely* for the purpose of writing down your experiences during meditation. In it, you will be recording your questions, experiences and insights received during short, focused meditations, preferably done on a daily basis. As stated before, the time and place of your meditations should remain fairly constant. It is beneficial to have a sacred space in which to do your spiritual work so that the integrity of the energy within it will remain constant and pure. This does not have to be a separate room; it can just as easily be a quiet corner of your bedroom or some other room of your dwelling that you clear for this purpose. Make sure it is a space that is comfortable and inviting. A small altar with items that are meaningful to you may be placed in the area. A blanket, along with pillows and a comfortable chair, should also be part of the space. It is preferable to sit for most meditations so that you will remain alert. However, if you feel it is more comfortable to lie down, you may do so. Meditation does no good if we resist it in any way; so by all means, be comfortable. Just remember the goal is to actively participate in the process, not fall asleep.

To begin, take out your special journal and open it to a fresh page. Enter the date at the top of the page. Close your eyes and take a deep breath. Center your energy in your heart chakra. Breathe into your heart and simply notice what is there. It may be light, airy energy, or it may be a heavy, dense feeling. Do not judge what you are feeling; simply notice it and breathe into it. Allow your heart chakra to expand as you continue to breathe. Now begin to formulate a question in your mind that you want to receive guidance on. This can be anything that you desire it to be. Perhaps you want to receive guidance on a specific situation or relationship that is currently confusing you. Or you want more understanding about certain areas of your spiritual growth. Whatever the inquiry, write it in question format in your journal. Be as specific as possible, but leave some room for flexibility in the answer to allow the guidance received to be exactly what it needs to be, unhampered by your expectations. (Note: The simpler the question, the better.) Examples of questions are: "What are the two most important areas I need to explore now concerning my spiritual growth?" "How may I use my talents and abilities in the best way now?' "What are three things I can do to connect more strongly with my purpose?"

Your guides, teachers, and angels will assist you in every way possible to receive the answers you most need to hear at the time. Because they are one with our higher consciousness, the guides will always speak to you in language that touches your soul. This is the language of unconditional love. Guides of a high vibration will always recognize and understand your concerns and personal life situations. They will do what they can to assist you in releasing old patterns that prevent you from moving forward.

After writing the question in your journal, prepare to do a short, focused meditation. It is best to do a meditation of only 10-15 minutes duration. I have found that the longer one stays in meditation, the easier it is to drift, which is non-productive in gaining inner awareness. Before entering meditation, set your intent to receive the guidance you most need now. The word "now" focuses energy in the present moment and brings it to a point of clarity for you. Remind your guides to come to you in a way that you will clearly understand. Finally, ask to remember all the wisdom imparted to you during the meditation.

Gently go into a meditative state. You may wish to use soft music that is conducive to expanded states of consciousness. Focus on your breath, allowing it to keep you centered in the moment. Any time you feel yourself beginning to drift, focus again on your breath and come back to the moment. The following is an exercise I have used with much success in connecting with my spirit guides and my higher self:

After focusing on your breath for a few moments, surround yourself in pure white light from head to toe. Feel the safety, comfort and love within the light. Let the cares of the day fall away. Imagine you are standing under a refreshing waterfall that is washing you clean of all stress, worry and concern. Repeat to yourself, "I am releasing all that is not love from my mind, body and entire auric field now. I am open to receive the very highest and best guidance from the wisdom of my soul." Feel yourself becoming more and more relaxed with each breath.

See in front of you a beautiful white column of light. This is the light connecting you to the Source of all being, wisdom and love. Gently step into this column of light and begin to feel yourself drifting higher and higher, lighter and freer. Allow yourself to experience the feeling of floating in the lightness of this energy as you drift higher still. Silently ask to be taken to a special place of wisdom where you will be in direct contact with your guides. This may be a garden, a temple, or a quiet room. Call upon all of your guides and invite them to join you in this place now. Ask that they come to you gently. Open your heart to welcome and receive your guides' presence. Feel your heart expanding as your receive their love and feel their touch.

Find a comfortable place to rest in your special place

of wisdom. Open your heart to receive the messages your guides are communicating in pictures, colors, words or feelings. Release and let go. Let your guides touch you with their unconditional love and assurance. Know you are one with them. Just be for a moment.

Now ask to receive a gift that has meaning for you in your life now. Open your hands to receive this gift, clutching it to your heart to feel its energy. If you do not understand its meaning, ask to know. You will receive an answer in words, images or feelings. Give thanks for the gift. Ask your guides if there are any final messages from them. Again, open your heart to receive and listen.

Now with your gift held closely to your heart, return to the white column of light. Gently come back down the column, returning to the present time and space. Move around, feeling your feet firmly upon the ground and your awareness back in the room. Breathe deeply and stretch.

Open your journal and begin to write down what you felt, heard and saw in your meditation. This is your direct experience of the time you have just spent with your guides and should be completely unfiltered by your judgment. If you saw color, write this down. If you sensed or saw a person or animal, describe them as clearly as you can. The important thing is to write down your experiences, allowing your inner senses to guide you in the process.

When you are done writing, open your journal to the question you asked before you went into meditation. Begin to write the answer to the question as it flows from your mind. The writing should come forth naturally and easily. Allow your hand to flow with the words that come into your awareness. Do not judge what you are receiving, and don't reread what you have already written. Instead, write until the flow stops. (You will know when this happens.) While writing, you may hear some of the words being communicated to you in your thoughts. Try to transcribe them exactly as you receive them.

Once you are finished writing, reread the material. Allow it to permeate your consciousness. What have you discovered? If you have followed your intuition, the information you received will not sound as if you wrote it personally; it will have a "higher" perspective than your personality. It will often be written in the second person, which uses the word "you." Our spiritual companions speak directly to us to emphasize or clarify a point. It's similar to someone saying, "You! Pay attention to this!" The writing will reflect your original intent in asking the question. That is, it will be as specific in nature and clarity as the question you originally posed. If the answers you received are too general, rewrite your question to make it more specific and repeat the exercise.

The value of receiving intuitive information lies in its guidance for your life. It is reflective of the larger picture, or overall scheme and purpose of your life. Prophecy, or the revelation of future events affecting your situation, may also be revealed in your writing because you are tuning into expanded states of awareness during meditation. You can receive prophecy by seeing clairvoyant images of the future, having a feeling about something that is going to happen, or hearing a word, phrase or sentence in your mind. Keep in mind that you have the ability to change your future because of free will. Prophecy is based on your present thoughts and pathway and changes if you change your thoughts and course of action.

This form of meditation can be done daily, weekly or whenever you want insight and clarification into a situation or challenge. It may also be done for the sole purpose of enlightenment on your spiritual pathway. It provides powerful guidance that comes from tapping into your intuition. Writing helps to bring this wisdom into your conscious awareness to make it recognizable and real. This is beneficial to spiritual growth because sometimes we become confused by the chatter of our analytical minds. The combination of meditation and journaling provides us with information seen through the loving perspective of our guides and our own higher selves. Another advantage of this process is the ability to do a retrospective of past journal writings to assess your patterns and growth. While reviewing your journal entries, you can ask yourself questions such as, "Where was I six months ago with this situation?" or "What do I do when faced with a similar challenge?" Experiment with the process. Above all else, make it enjoyable! Sometimes the information that comes through in the writing is humorous, particularly if our joy guides are involved. A sign of true spiritual growth is when we can laugh at the dramas and traumas of our lives.

Recognizing and Strengthening the Connection with Your Guides

Here is a short, simple meditation that you can do to strengthen your connection with your guides and your own intuition.

Get comfortable, close your eyes and visually surround yourself with pure, white light. Imagine the light encompassing your whole being, from head to toe, as it pours into your crown at the top of your head, and spreads throughout your entire body. Feel the safety, warmth and compassion contained within the light as it radiates through each and every cell. Silently ask that the light strengthen and heal you for the highest good of your soul. Affirm that you are asking to connect with those who come from the light realms of love and healing.

Now focus your attention on your heart area. Feel the light emanating from this center. Begin to breathe through the heart, feeling it expand and becoming lighter with each breath. Think of a loved one in your life and envision his or her face. Look into the eyes and send love to that person. Feel the love being returned to you as it is magnified a thousandfold. As you are experiencing this circle of love, ask that a guide who comes in love and compassion draw near to you now. Ask that the experience be gentle and non-threatening. Allow yourself to open to the full possibilities of connecting and touching with your spirit guide.

Ask the guide if there is something you need to know now for your spiritual growth. Ask that this be clearly and lovingly communicated to you. Ask to remember it. This may be a word, a symbol, an image or a feeling. Open your heart to accept and give thanks for the wisdom imparted.

Now focus your attention on your physical body, feeling your feet firmly on the ground. Bring your attention back to the physical space you're in and open your eyes.

What were your experiences? Were you able to connect with your guide? Sensing your guides' presence can happen in various ways: feelings of unconditional love and peace; tingling sensations around your shoulders and head; hearing your name softly spoken; sensing a gentle touch on your body or seeing a color or image that represents your guide. A combination of these "signals" may also be used by your guide to communicate with you. Each time that you recognize your guide, the connection becomes stronger.

Persistence and patience are indispensable in the process of intuitive development. Many people feel as if they "should" be seeing someone or something when they meditate. Do not be discouraged if you aren't seeing anything. Feeling is just as valid. Your guides will come to you in the way you are most receptive to them. The best tip to follow is to stay open to what you are receiving. I have met with clients who have described their guides' physical appearance to a tee. On the other hand, I have known people who simply feel their guides' loving presence at certain times. Either way is perfectly acceptable in terms of our spiritual growth. There is no right or wrong way to connect with spiritual companions. As stated earlier, don't feel as if you have to know the names of your guides. Many guides are recognized by their vibration, not their names. Some of them consider a name to be reflective of the ego and therefore limiting.

If you wish to have your guides come to your awareness in a particular way, ask them to do so. Usually, they will try to communicate with you on your terms. After all, what good is the relationship if you can't relate?

Can I Use a Ouija Board To Connect With My Guides?

Tuning into your guides should never be a frightening experience. Most guides would rather you not be aware of them at all than to scare you. This defeats the purpose of the connection—which is precisely why I advise clients not to use a Ouija board to connect with their guides. Unless one is experienced in practicing discernment during psychic exercises, the Ouija board can act as a portal for manipulative astral entities to grab your undivided attention (something they crave). These entities usually reside in the lower levels of the spirit world, which are closest to the earth. Some of them have chosen to stay close to the earth because of unfinished business from a previous life. They are amused when they can trick or manipulate those who don't use discernment when opening to psychic energies. Many people who use a device like a Oiuja board are uninformed about the spirit world and fail to use adequate discernment in the process of "tuning" in. If a manipulative spirit is attracted into their home or auric field, he or she may not be so easy to get rid of. Often, these entities are happy to take up residence with those who will give them the attention they want.

I once did a reading for a woman who was seeking

guidance on how to get rid of an entity that had taken control of her home. She told me that the entity would take hold of her arm and lead her around to different areas of the house, presumably to communicate with her in some way. She was very afraid of what he would "force" her to do next. I asked her if she had ever used a Ouija board for entertainment. She admitted that she had done so several times in an attempt to communicate with spirits. I suggested that she set very firm boundaries with her "guest" by telling him in no uncertain terms that he needed to leave her home and go to the light. She was confused about why this had happened to her. I explained that she had unintentionally invited the entity in by using the portal of the board because she hadn't set clear boundaries with her intent in contacting the spirit world. I told her that it is extremely important that one uses discernment in all matters of spiritual awakening, particularly when tuning into other realms of consciousness.

Generally, to attract pleasant experiences during meditation, it is a good rule of thumb to be in an emotionally balanced state before connecting with your guides. Avoid using drugs or alcohol before meditation because they tend to weaken the aura, and possibly leave you vulnerable to the influence of manipulative entities.

An Exercise to See Your Guide

Many people desire to see their guides through clairvoyance. Try this "viewing" technique the next time you meditate. (Note: it is important to be deeply relaxed and stress-free for this particular exercise. Don't attempt it if you are overly tired, frustrated or anxious because these states block your higher sense perception. Also, do not be discouraged if you don't immediately see your guide. It takes practice and patience.):

After going into meditation and becoming deeply relaxed, see a blank painter's canvas in front of you. Silently ask one of your guides, one who comes in light and love, to appear to you on this canvas. As you hold the focus, allow your inner eye to shift downward to the bottom of the canvas. Breathe deeply as you let your inner eye slowly move up the length of the canvas, from bottom to top. You may start to receive the impression of a figure forming on the canvas. Greet your guide with love and welcome him or her. Feel your guide's form with your inner senses. It may initially seem or appear fuzzy. What is your impression?

Now go back to the bottom of the canvas and start visualizing, from the feet up, the image of your guide. It is easiest if you allow the image to be filled in this way, starting at the bottom of the canvas. What does your guide's feet look like? Is he/she barefoot? If not, what type of foot covering does he/she wear? Make a mental note of this as you move on to scan the rest of the image.

Slowly move your inner eye up from the feet to look at the body. What type of clothing is the guide wearing? Is your guide of a particular nationality or ethnic origin? What does his/her body look like? Heavy or slim? Is he/she carrying or holding anything? Again, make a mental note of this and continue to scan the image as it appears to you.

Now move on to the head and the face. Look into the eyes of your guide. What soul qualities do you sense? Study any outstanding details of the face as it appears to you. Note the hairstyle and color. Breathe in and again focus upon the entire image, from toe to head. Breathe in again and slowly come back to the present time and space. Journal your experiences immediately after coming out of this meditation so you will not forget any of them. Optimally, you may wish to draw the image of your guide as it appeared to you. Remember, do not judge the information you receive!

Keeping the Communication Open

Once you have established communication with your guides, you can engage in internal dialogue any time you wish. After a while, you will become very familiar with the ways your guides speak to you. Don't be discouraged if you don't receive immediate answers to all your questions; sometimes we have to simply wait things out during intense periods of our spiritual growth. Our guides give us breathing room to discover things on our own. To give us time to adjust, they may step back when we need to incorporate new growth patterns into our consciousness. This doesn't mean they have deserted us; they are simply supporting us in our pathway by allowing us to experience and integrate our lessons.

Sometimes, our guides communicate nothing except a sense of unconditional love, which you will feel by tuning into your feelings during meditation. When you acknowledge and return their love, you strengthen the ties that bind you with your spiritual companions.

13

LIFE GOES ON:
THE SPIRIT WORLD

"My mother passed into spirit several years ago. Why hasn't she communicated with my family? Does that mean she doesn't care about us anymore?" "How do I communicate with my loved ones in spirit?" "What should I expect when it is my time to cross over?" "What do we do in the spirit world?" Clients ask me these and many other questions when they come for readings.

Many people today are expressing a keen interest in life after death. I believe that the current popularity of mediumship, especially on TV, has come about as a result of people seeking to comprehend the meaning of life and death from a deeper, more spiritually centered perspective than in the past. Coupled with this is an increasing realization that the responsibility for the quality and direction of our lives, including the way we choose to die, lies solely with us. With this understanding, people are discovering that they need not fear death because it is a natural transition in life and that our spirit lives on.

Through my communication with many spirits, I have received direct information regarding the nature of life in the spirit worlds. Most importantly, I have witnessed firsthand how this information can be of great comfort and healing to the one seeking to connect with a loved one in spirit. Years of unresolved grief, guilt, doubt and fear can oftentimes be dissolved in a single session in which the loved one comes through to express and acknowledge the survival of his or her soul after death and deliver messages of love. The unconditionally loving perspective communicated by those in the spirit world can be extremely helpful to loved ones on earth—helping them to heal and bring closure to their loss.

What is life like in the spirit world? What do we do once we're there? Do we eat, sleep, work and play? What does the spirit world look like? How do we decide when to come back into a physical body? Let's take a look at the spirit world—a world as wonderfully rich and diverse in every way as earth. (The gracious spirits who have come through during my sessions have revealed most of this information to me. Other parts have been communicated to me by my spirit guides—especially my joy guide, Rolf.)

Transition and Adjustment to the World of Spirit

When we make transition to the spirit world, our loved ones in spirit along with our spirit guides, come to greet us and help us move through a tunnel of light that connects the earth and the spirit world. Once we have made this transition, we are given the opportunity through the replay of our Akashic Records, or Book of Life, to instantly see all of our lifetimes, full and complete, in panoramic vision. During this process, we re-experience everything in our most recent life, no matter how insignificant it seemed to us at the time, including what effect our life had on others. We feel the emotions of others who have been in our life, and the significance of the relationships we've had with them. Although we are normally unaware of it, the life we lead touches many other people, some of whom we may never meet. I call this the "ripple" effect because it is similar to the waves that are formed when a pebble is thrown into the water. Our spirit guides and angels help us through the emotional "hot spots" we encounter during our life review, during which we make an assessment of the spiritual work we still need to do. Based on this assessment and the recommendation of our guides, we choose the most appropriate pathway that meets our needs.

A word needs to be said concerning our thoughts and expectations before leaving our physical bodies. Because our thoughts create everything in our lives, they automatically draw us to a place in the spirit world that closely matches their vibratory frequency. If we regularly hold thoughts of a relatively low vibration, such as anger or fear, we will find ourselves in the spirit world at a similarly dense level. (These levels tend to be darker in terms of light intensity than the higher ones.) On the other hand, if we are primarily happy and loving, we gravitate to the lighter levels. Because the world of spirit is primarily made up of thought forms, we will, upon passing, go to the level of thought that most closely matches our predominate state of mind. Our expectations concerning the process of dying, the afterlife and any religious beliefs also determine where we go once we have had our life review. For example, are we filled with fear about what will happen to us when we leave our physical bodies? Do we adhere to stringent religious ideas about heaven and hell? Do we believe we are more than our physical bodies? Or have we been confused about exactly *what* we believe? The answers to these questions will largely determine the ease with which we pass from our body and the nature of our new space in the spirit world. I strongly recommend that people examine their beliefs about these crucial issues long *before* physical death to facilitate a smooth and peaceful transition.

If we don't believe we are more than our body, we may remain attached to it long after death has occurred. This is sometimes the case in cemetery "hauntings," where a spirit is seen hovering near a grave. These are spirits who are not aware of their own death. As incredulous as it sounds, these souls may wander the earth for years, trying to live the life they passed from. Some of these spirits attempt to inhabit their former houses and consequently create a haunting. The best way to help these souls is to tell them that they have passed out of their body and now need to go through the tunnel of light to the spirit world. Most are grateful for this assistance in moving on because they are tired of wandering on the earth and desire to rest.

Fear of death can also prevent us from experiencing a smooth transition into the spirit world. Fear traps us into believing that we must hold onto our earthly life because we don't know what will happen to us after we pass from our body. It causes us to struggle against making the natural transition of death when the time arrives for us to do so. The more knowledge we have of what to expect in the spirit world, the less likely we are to let fear of death paralyze us.

Going Home

After our life review, we go through a period of adjustment that helps us become acclimated to the conditions of the spirit world. This is done in a "decompression" chamber in which we can adapt to once again experiencing the expansiveness of our spirit without it being condensed into a physical body. Because our spirit bodies (also called the astral body) are made up primarily of our thoughts and emotions, they hold no weight or mass. As stated before, our astral body travels in the astral dimension during sleep yet remains attached to the physical body by a thin cord of energy. At death, the astral body separates completely from the physical body and hovers above it before making transition through the tunnel of light leading to the spirit world. The energy that comprises our astral body is so finely dispersed that what would be considered impossible in the physical world is routine in the spirit world. For example, it is possible for our astral body to "walk through" walls (I have seen this happen.) Within our spirit body are receptors for senses that enable us to see, hear, and feel in the spirit world. These astral senses help us to navigate within the spirit world much as our physical senses do on earth. During sleep, these senses relay information to us from the dream state.

After we become comfortable with our spirit body, we are given the opportunity to speak with spirit counselors about any unresolved emotional issues we have carried from our most recent life. They encourage and support us, without judgment, to release any thought patterns that prevent us from reaching a peaceful place in the spirit world. Although we have free will, it is to our benefit to release emotional baggage that keeps us magnetically glued to the lower levels of the spirit world. If anger, grief, resentment or sadness were not adequately resolved while we were in physical form, they must be re-examined once we have made passage. Spiritual growth does not stop in the spirit world; we continue to learn and experience just as we have done on earth. The only difference is the absence of our physical body.

Incidentally, since we no longer have a physical body to consider, there really is no need for us to eat or sleep. However, some souls choose to continue to go through the thought processes of doing these things. After complete adjustment to one's spirit body is made, the desire to do this usually falls away.

No Time or Space

One of the biggest adjustments we make after leaving the physical world is the release of our perceptions of both time and space. (The earth plane is the only dimension in which these concepts exist.) We may spend the equivalent of many earth years in one vibratory level in the spirit world until we are ready to move to another. Or we may choose to come back to earth to continue our learning in physical form. In both the spirit world and in our earthly lives, we have as long as we need to assimilate the spiritual lessons necessary for our growth. What is not learned in one lifetime will be learned in another. Or we may choose to learn the same lesson in the world of spirit.

Like time, the concept of space is unknown after we cross over. Different levels of the spirit world are not separated by space as we know it, but by the frequency of their vibration. Our spirit bodies, unlike our physical ones, are expansive and unrestricted by the denseness of the material world. One of the most challenging adjustments that newly crossed spirits have to make is the realization that their thoughts can take them wherever they desire. In the spirit world, we need only think about being in a certain place, condition, or situation—and presto! Instantly we are in it. The old adage, "Be careful what you ask for, you may get it" applies to this phenomenon of instant manifestation. Many spirits who cross over have to learn to control their thoughts to create what they want. Our guides and trained counselors assist us in adjusting to these conditions. We may even choose to take classes in thought control to re-learn the power of our thoughts and how they create our reality.

Without the restriction of space, we can easily be in the most remote geographical location in the world in the length of time it takes to think about that place. We can then think about another place we might like to visit, and be there as quickly as we could think about it. Free from the confines of time and space, we can visit any place that we can think of, including the cosmos. The only limitations are our own thoughts.

What Does the Spirit World Look Like?

There are many levels to the spirit planes and each one is slightly different than the others. The ones closest to the earth are relatively dense in vibration compared to the ones furthest away. In addition, each level is reflective of the vibration of thought of its inhabitants.

Some spirits that have come through in sessions describe the light that prevails in any given realm of spirit. In the lower levels, the light is relatively dim; in the higher levels, it is brighter. This light is reflective of the vibration of thought and consciousness prevailing in the particular level. Generally the less dense a thought is, the brighter the light and vice versa.

As stated before, we naturally go to the level in the spirit world that exactly matches our cumulative thoughts over a lifetime. A majority of people make transition into the mid-spirit planes, which are similar to our surroundings on the physical plane. The familiarity of these regions allows us to adjust more easily to our transition. There are spirit houses, schools, libraries and churches. There are lush green countrysides with clear streams. Recreational areas complete with sports arenas, parks and spirit animals are also common. Basically, anything you can imagine that exists on earth exists in the spirit world, but without physical form. This brings up an important point regarding the nature of reality. The spirit world is just as real in every sense as the physical one. Both are real in the sense that they exist based on the collective consciousness of the inhabitants. The primary difference in the two worlds is the relative vibration of the thought energy that is present. The spirit world vibrates at a higher intensity than the physical one.

The universal law of resonance (like attracts like) applies in the spirit world, which means that we will be with like-minded souls who share our thoughts and beliefs. In addition, it is common for groups of souls in the mid-levels to live together in homes that are built by thought. Often these houses are similar or identical to the ones a spirit lived in on earth. There has been speculation among Spiritualists (those who believe in and prove the continuity of life) that houses do not exist in the higher planes of the spirit world because inhabitants there have shed their need to identify with earth. Whether this is the case or not does not matter as much as the cohesiveness of similar groups of souls who exist in *all* of the levels.

Most spirits choose to be with their family members immediately following transition into the spirit plane. This includes married couples who desire to reunite after crossing over. On the other hand, some souls may choose to move on from a particular relationship because it has afforded maximum learning. Others may choose to continue a relationship in the spirit world because more healing needs to occur. The truth is that no relationship *ever* ends and we are eternally united with one another in all of our relationships. It is the illusion of separateness we have on earth that leads us to believe our loved ones have "left" us when in reality they are inextricably linked to us by the binding ties of love. We need only think of our loved ones and they instantly feel our love.

Color and Sound in the Spirit World

One of the most remarkable qualities of the spirit world is the intensity and vibrancy of its colors. Beautiful displays of any color imaginable comprise the middle and higher levels. The lower levels contain more subdued color, some of them being almost gray. In many of my sessions I see the communicating spirits standing or sitting in fields of bright, green grass surrounded by exquisitely colored flowers. In one session, the client's mother in spirit said that she wanted her family to know she was in a beautiful place and no longer had to worry about mowing the lawn! The grass was always one perfect length.

In meditations, I have seen the vibrant colors of the spirit world, especially in hues of bright violet and green. There really are no earthly colors to compare to the beauty of those in the spirit world. It is as if the light of the Divine flows directly through them, illuminating them and increasing their intensity. My guides and teachers once informed me that color is used to heal spirits who have crossed over from illnesses that have emotionally drained them. There are hospitals that exist for such purposes and often will be the first stop for spirits who have passed from a debilitating illness such as cancer or AIDS. My guides have explained that many experiments are currently being done in the spirit world to use color to assist these souls and others in healing. One of these involves the use of a color "cocoon" which wraps a spirit in a particular color to absorb its healing vibration. For example, some spirits are wrapped in vibrant green to help them regain emotional balance. Some of this research in the spirit world is being channeled to earth through alternative healing practitioners who use it in complementary healing modalities such as color therapy.

Sound exists in the world of spirit and is similar to our physical auditory sense. The music of the heavenly spheres can be heard in spirit churches and special concerts, some of which are given by the angels. Because our spirit ears are not the same as our physical ones, we mainly perceive sounds through telepathy, which is thought transfer. According to my guides, this means we receive thought vibrations through feeling centers in our spirit body. We perceive sound when it affects these centers.

How do we speak to one another in the astral levels? Telepathy is the way that spirits communicate with one another. Mediums commonly receive the thought impressions of spirits when they communicate. Our astral senses—clairvoyance, clairaudience, and clairsentience—are specially geared to receive this type of communication and function independently of our five physical senses. These inner senses are constantly transmitting information to us from the higher vibratory worlds of spirit. Many people ignore or "write off" these messages as figments of imagination, when in fact, these messages are transmitting significant information to them—such as communication from loved ones in spirit and prophecy.

If you have ever had the experience of hearing a voice in your head as you were falling asleep at night, you have most likely experienced clairaudience. Some people have heard actual spirit voices as they are being sent from the communicating spirit. When this happens to me, I notice that the voice is distorted and far away, as if it is emanating from outside of my head. Spirit voices sound disjointed and at times, I must admit, rather uncanny. In the spirit world, communication is more direct and cohesive, mainly due to the fact that one is not traversing a dimension to be heard. Communication is quicker and more concise; a single thought may encompass an entire concept, idea or feeling. I have experienced this "consolidated" communication in sessions when a spirit impresses its thoughts upon my mind. A large amount of information can be transferred in this manner. Telepathy is a most efficient method of communication!

The world of spirit is filled with a diversity of sounds. Choirs of singers, symphonies and orchestras exist to uplift, inspire and soothe us much as they do here. Musicians who were famous during their earthly lives continue to use their talents to inspire those on earth who compose and perform. This is accomplished mainly through inspiration from those in the spirit world.

Our Spiritual Growth Continues After Physical Death

We choose to have many experiences in our physical bodies for the advancement and refinement of our souls, each one removing another layer of the veil that separates us from our innate divine perfection. In between lifetimes, we spend time in the spirit world, which is our real home. It is real in the sense that the illusion of our duality and separation from our divine nature, which is *unreal,* does not exist. This does not mean that one plane of existence is preferable to another; each offers us the opportunity to grow. The existence of duality on earth is a necessary ingredient in our soul's progression, providing many chances for us to learn by experiencing contrasts.

Illness and disease do not exist in the spirit world. What does exist is further opportunity to learn spiritual lessons under different conditions. If we leave unfinished business (karma) behind when we make transition from our physical life, we have ample opportunity to continue and perhaps conclude that business in the spirit world. This can be done in many different ways. The following is a short discussion of only several of the means by which we continue our spiritual growth in the spirit world. Many others exist, depending on our individual needs and karma.

After making transition, many spirits choose to rest and reflect upon their earthly life. Some spirits engage in the same pastimes and recreational activities as they enjoyed on earth and may even assist us in our enjoyment of recreation. In one of my sessions, a departed husband told his widow that she was pulling back too far on her golf swing! Some spirits, particularly those who have lived long lives or done hard labor, stay in this period of relaxation for what amounts to many earth years.

Eventually, we feel the desire to resume our learning and seek the means to continue our lessons in the spirit world. Some souls go to spirit schools for special types of learning, such as teaching others both in the spirit world and on earth. Some become better prepared to assist others from the spirit world in the fields of medicine or education by studying these subjects in depth. There are probably as many schools and universities that exist in the spirit world as here on earth, and with much the same purpose: to prepare people to serve humanity. According to my guide Rolf, there are even schools and training programs that teach souls how to be spirit guides. These schools are rigorous because of the amount of responsibility involved. Based on our decision and our guides' advice, we choose to become involved in these advanced studies so we may serve others with our knowledge. In this respect, the spirit world is much the same as the physical one.

Employment opportunities are available for us if we want them. Although there is rarely an exchange of money, the experience and period of service is recorded in our Book of Life. Some souls choose to become involved in pursuits similar to what they did on earth; others opt to expand their horizons by doing something totally different from their earthly occupations. Libraries, schools, hospitals and churches that exist in the spirit world offer countless opportunities for service and learning.

Specialized positions of service abound in the spirit world. These include spirits who train to rescue souls who cry out for assistance from the lower levels of the spirit world where the dense vibration of their thoughts has attracted them. When spirits express a desire to change their thoughts, the "rescuers" come in to lift them into a healing vibration in the light of the higher planes. Because the lower planes are very dense and fear-based in thought vibration, this is a mission that requires courage and strength of character. Sometimes the angels act as beacons of light to lead both spirits to the higher planes where light prevails and healing takes place.

There are spirits who help those in the process of making transition through the tunnel of light and are having a difficult time doing so. Spirit hospitals are staffed with those who assist newly arriving souls who have suffered a debilitating illness before passing from their bodies and are in need of emotional and spiritual rehabilitation. Souls who have studied theology and have pastoral abilities head spirit churches of every denomination. Counselors are trained on all levels of the spirit world to help those in need of emotional healing, which is a deciding factor in a spirit's passage to the higher levels of existence.

One of the most highly revered positions is that of teacher. After we cross over, there is a strong emphasis placed on learning. Teachers of all types are in demand because they have dedicated themselves to the advancement of those seeking knowledge to serve humanity in some capacity. There are lectures presented on any topic imaginable in universities and huge libraries that store the many records of humankind's accomplishments, triumphs and spiritual consciousness throughout history. Any period in human evolution may be viewed instantly through an "energy scope" (viewing portal that replays thought vibrations) with the approval of the attending librarian.

A specialized position in the spirit world that requires sincere dedication and determination to serve others is that of spirit guide to those on earth. Because these spirits have had prior association with the one they are guiding from former lifetimes, both souls share similar spiritual lessons and purpose. It is a great honor and privilege to be chosen as a guide and requires emotional detachment, compassion, patience and a large amount of unconditional love. Rolf has told me that all who apply for the job are not accepted because the screening process is rigorous with many tests to determine one's eligibility.

Clearly, there is much to do, see and learn in the spirit world where we can stay as long as we desire, experiencing all it has to offer us. When the time is right, and we feel that we have temporarily learned all we can on that side of life, we once again meet with our guides and decide when we shall return to the great classroom of earth to continue our journey and further our soul's enrichment in the physical dimension.

The Eternal Nature of Love

If there is a solitary message that almost all spirits communicate in sessions it is that love never dies. Time and again, I have been able to bring that simple yet powerful message to those seeking to make contact with their loved ones on the other side of life. It is our core essence of love that binds and connects us eternally to these relationships. Ironically, we may actually be closer in heart and mind to our loved ones after their passing, because earthly constraints such as time and space no longer separate us. Those whom we have loved as spouses, family members, friends and pets continue to send us unconditional love, prayers and healing energy from the spirit world.

In many sessions, I have seen and felt the essence of prayer sent by a client's loved one in spirit. This is especially true when there is emotional distress or illness within the family. Our loved ones in spirit regularly send us prayers for our emotional and physical healing. Sometimes they will come to soothe and reassure us when we are experiencing a frightening surgery or a medical emergency. Many spirits express concern for family members who may have recently been hospitalized and will communicate this during a session. They are also with us during joyous occasions such as birth. I once did a session in which a client's deceased mother wanted her to know she had been at her side when she gave birth. She laughed upon hearing this, adding that she felt her mother's presence there the whole time.

People often want to know how our loved ones' presence can be felt in times of grief and emotional or physical pain. Most commonly it is through gentle thought impressions in which they let us know they are aware of our fear, discomfort or pain. These thoughts come over us as feelings of love, comfort, and warmth. Sometimes we may feel a light touch upon our shoulders, smell our loved one's favorite perfume, or have a mysterious phone call with no one on the other end of the line. These are all ways in which spirits communicate their nearby presence and the awareness of our thoughts and feelings.

Another important message that comes through from the spirit world is the reality of the continuity of life after physical death. Many spirits wish to simply be acknowledged and remembered in a session, often by bringing through their name, initial or other identifying characteristics. "Yes, I'm still alive!" is the essence of these communications. Sometimes they will speak about the nature of the spirit world, but most often they will give confirmation of their lives on earth—such as favorite pastimes, childhood memories, and specific information on how they passed from their physical bodies. It is very important to them to be recognized by the client in the session so that they may communicate the reality of the afterlife and their continued survival.

It is always a surprise to the client when an unexpected spirit comes through in a session. In many instances, clients receive confirmation of communication from a neighbor, a person they cared for, or a distant relative or friend who desires to get a message through to someone the client has contact with. In the last case, spirits consider a medium to be a lifeline to reach loved ones who aren't sensitive to their thoughts and will often provide names or connecting circumstances to validate their messages. We may even hear from spirits we have known through our work.

Ruth is a critical-care nurse who came for a session in which she wanted to hear from her father. After opening with a prayer, I immediately began receiving thought impressions from Ruth's father. He communicated his passing from lung cancer and information about recent family happenings, which Ruth confirmed. As he continued to speak, I could feel the presence of another spirit who wanted to reach Ruth. I began to sense a gray-haired woman in her 70's. She gave no name, but spoke of her passing from breast cancer. "I just wanted to say thank you for taking such good care of me when I was sick," she said. "You helped to ease my pain and make it easier for me to cross over." Ruth had no idea who this woman was. After a few moments, she recalled a woman with breast cancer named Naomi, who had been one of her patients in critical-care. "I received a thank-you card for caring for Naomi from her family," she said tearfully, "but I never expected to hear directly from her."

Last, but certainly not least, are the messages spirits communicate to provide healing and closure for their loved ones who remain. In a recent session, Connie wanted to make contact with her daughter who had passed tragically from a car crash. When she came through, the young woman delivered many messages, but one with special significance: a direct plea for her mother to release the tremendous guilt and responsibility she felt for her passing. "It was my time to go," she said. "There was nothing else that you could have done." At this point in the session, the mother began to cry, tearfully admitting that for years she had indeed felt a heavy burden of guilt surrounding her daughter's passing. Although the reasons for this were never made clear to me, I am certain that a remarkable healing took place that day for both mother and daughter.

Reassurance

Perhaps the greatest lesson we can learn from understanding the spirit world is one that concerns one of humankind's deepest fears: dying. Since all fear originates from a lack of understanding, it stands to reason that the more we understand about the nature of the spirit world and what we can expect when we get there, the more reassurance we have of making a smooth transition when our time arrives. The spirits who have made relatively easy passage through the tunnel of light and adjusted quickly to life in the spirit world are those who have prepared themselves beforehand to make the journey. The more we think and plan for our transition, the better. In order to do this, we must release as much emotional baggage as we can while we are still here. Feelings of guilt, fear, anger and resentment can be compared to holding the vibration of mud, as far as the density of our emotional state is concerned. Loved ones who have come through in sessions I have done with people holding onto this sort of emotional clutter usually prompt them to re-evaluate things and let go. The more healing we can do here, the less we have to do after our passage. Some spirits have come through in sessions to urge loved ones to "clean up" their unfinished business before it's too late, because that is exactly what happened to them. Do what you can today, they say, before you have to drag it over here. There is no time like the present to heal.

In the future, it will be commonplace for people to communicate on a regular basis with those in the spirit world. The evolution of our spiritual consciousness will create a blending between earth and higher dimensions of spirit. Mediumship will no longer be subjected to the intense scrutiny of debunkers because it will no longer be necessary to prove the reality of the afterlife and the survival of our souls after physical death. We will *know* it to be true. Speaking with the spirit world will be as easy as calling someone on the phone. People will no longer fear making the transition back home because it will be considered a natural extension of the life they have always known. Children will not be ridiculed for seeing and entertaining invisible playmates. We will release concepts of death based in fear. We will joyfully claim our spiritual identities as divine beings who never die. We will *understand.*

Exercise for Self–Enlightenment

If you could change one thing about your life today, what would it be? How might changing this contribute to your healing? What is necessary in practical terms for you to make this change happen? Take one positive step today to realize this change.

14

PARTING THE VEIL: EMBRACING AND CARRYING YOUR LIGHT

The material world challenges us in many ways to stretch our boundaries of limitation and release fears that prevent us from realizing our true identity of love. Before we awaken spiritually, we "sleepwalk" behind the veil of illusion that separates us from the recognition of God within us. As we walk the pathway of self-illumination on earth, we find ourselves alternately standing on mountaintops of light and in valleys of darkness. At times, we stand at crossroads of indecision, unsure of the direction we need to take. The only constancy in our journey rests in the awareness of the light of God that resides in our hearts. No matter what illusion we invent for ourselves, the eternal truth of our divine connection remains intact.

In the journey of self-discovery, we find ourselves asking questions such as, "What is the next step on my pathway?" "How do I make changes in my life now that I know what needs to be changed?" and "How can I use my spiritual understanding to help others?" Paradoxically, the answers lie within our asking of the questions. The fact that we have even asked the questions indicates that we are ready and willing to receive the insights that lead us to the answers that are right for us at that moment. Because the universe rushes to fill a void, (a question is a void in our consciousness), we are assured direction from universal sources through our internal voice of intuition. Accessing this voice connects us with our divine blueprint and our soul's sacred purpose.

All Pathways Lead Us Home

Our knowledge of God increases with our knowledge of self; there is no separation between the two. Our journey of self-discovery takes us down many pathways, each of which leads to the destination of home, our pure identity of being one with Spirit. This "knowingness" of the light within makes us invulnerable to the illusions of fear and separation. In the light of Spirit, *all* pathways are valid and necessary for growth. Staying stuck in judgment of our or others' choices in life prevents us from experiencing the magnificent diversity of God. For one day, dare to be totally accepting of everything and everyone in your life, no matter what the circumstances. Realize that each person on earth expresses and reflects the sublime beauty of the Divine. Keep moving forward to eagerly experience the joy of the unfolding journey as it reveals itself to you moment by moment.

In the Joy Of the Moment

In the last year, I have attracted many circumstances emphasizing the lesson of patience. Frustrated, I struggled with these situations until I began to understand that spiritual growth does not consist of a final destination; it is a journey in which we slowly uncover the light within us to reveal our eternal connection with God. I have discovered that spiritual enlightenment is not an endgame. *Playing* is what counts; not winning. My need to separate, categorize and prioritize everything in my life is giving way to acceptance of the revelation of each moment as part of the "plan."

Staying in the moment means we release expectation of the way things *should* be. It enables us to fully experience our feelings and acknowledge the strength of our soul. The moment gives us the opportunity to reinvent ourselves through exerting our free will and provides us with the assurance of constant renewal by the power of our choices. The expression, "Seize the day," captures the essence of our ability to find power and strength in the time of NOW. We must not rest on the laurels of our past or allow our expectations of the future to deter us from claiming the rewards contained in the present moment.

Fear cannot exist in the power of the present moment because it is the product of concentration on the past or the future. If we are in the power of the moment, we are in neither the past nor future. My kundalini yoga instructor once told me that it is impossible for love and fear to exist in our heart at the same time when we focus on the miracle of our breath. Each breath we take connects us with God in the moment of NOW as we fill our lungs with *prana*, universal life-sustaining energy, which emanates directly from God. To reconnect with our divine source, we need only focus on our breath. It is very difficult to allow fear to control us when we literally *inspire* God.

The Gift Of You

You are the sole proprietor of your soul. No one on earth is *you*. Realize that your uniqueness enables you to give the gift of yourself to the world, which is something that is desperately needed. In a discussion about various types of employment, a favorite teacher once said, "No one on earth can do your job like you do." Our contribution to the world through a career, hobby, volunteer work or any other way is special in that it contains our individual interpretation of God. Although there really is "nothing new under the sun," old things can be done in new ways that introduce greater levels of understanding and healing to the world.

Carrying your light into the world means walking through your fears of rejection, failure, and unworthiness. We cannot expect to be a beacon of light for others when our own light is hidden beneath a veil of dark self-loathing and fear. The world we live in today is starving for healing of all kinds. One look around reveals that our world is capable of operating in a better way. Despite living in a technologically advanced society, people today hunger for deeper meaning in their lives. Dissatisfied with pure materialism without spiritual basis, we are turning inward to find the real treasures that reside only within our soul. We are awakening to the potential of expanding our consciousness to alleviate poverty, war, hatred and intolerance. Our sacred partnership with Mother Earth must be renewed and healed.

Our personal expression of God is our gift to the world. It's been said many times that one voice *does* make a difference. A single light can dissolve a sea of darkness. In a lifetime, we affect many others, some of whom we may never meet. Often, we remain unaware of the impact our life, words or actions have had on others until we cross over into spirit and review our life. It is then that we see the effect a kind word or generous deed had on another.

Those in the spirit world consistently bring messages of hope that help us to release judgment, embrace forgiveness and see the larger scope of life. At the heart of these messages is love—the tie that binds all together. The value of any message lies in its ability to help us change our life in some way. Knowledge, in and of itself, is meaningless unless it improves our quality of life. It is what we do with the knowledge that makes the difference. When we share our knowledge with others to heal and empower them, it strengthens our connection with God. When we offer healing to the world, we ultimately heal ourselves.

Daily, step into the garden of your soul. Nourish and forgive yourself and others with unconditional love. Realize that the splendor of your spirit is needed in the world to make it a better place. Stand in your power and live boldly from your Truth.

Resources

Talking to Heaven by James Van Praagh, published by Dutton (the Penguin group), New York.

Opening to Channel by Sanaya Roman and Duane Packer, published by H. J. Kramer, Inc, Tilburn, Ca.

The Power of Your Subconscious Mind by Dr. Joseph Murphy, published by Prentice-Hall, Englewood Cliffs, N. J.

Creating True Prosperity by Shakti Gawain, published by New World Library, Novato, Ca.

The Sevenfold Journey: Reclaiming Mind, Body & Spirit Through the Chakras by Anodea Judith and Selene Vega, published by the Crossing Press, Freedom, Ca.

Through Time Into Healing by Brian L. Weiss, M.D., published by Simon & Shuster, New York.

You Can Heal Your Life by Louise Hay, published by Hayhouse, Carlsbad, Ca.

Glossary of Metaphysical Terms

Acceleration—in spiritual terms, the speeding up of an individual's awareness of his/her divine mission, purpose and connection. This usually comes about as a result of an increase in the vibration and frequency of the crown chakra.

Affirmations—positive statements of truth that resonate with the innate perfection of the soul. They are verbalized, thought, or written for the purpose of attracting similar thought forms to the individual in the healing process.

Akashic Records—also called "The Book of Life." They are the sum total of a soul's experiences from the beginning of time. The collective records exist in the world of spirit and are guarded by special "Keepers of the Records." An individual's guardian angel watches over his/her record through successive lifetimes.

Angels—messengers of the Divine who have never been in a physical body, yet assist humankind in many and varied ways. There are numerous legions of angels, each of which carries a specific healing quality to uplift humans. (See the section on angels in the chapter "Spirit Consciousness: Angels, Healers, Teachers, and Other Spirit Guides.")

Ascended Masters—souls who have completed their lessons

on the earth plane and have balanced and met all karma. Jesus Christ, Krishna, and Buddha are examples.

Astral Body—also called the "emotional body." The third energy body in vibratory density after the physical and etheric. When we sleep, the astral body naturally separates from the physical body and travels the astral plane of consciousness. It is also the body that "crosses over" when we experience physical death.

Astral Plane—the fourth dimension of existence. It is commonly referred to as the spirit world or the 'Other Side." It is the plane we visit at night when dreaming and where we go when we make transition from physical life.

Aura—the invisible (to the physical eye) energetic reflection of an individual's thoughts and feelings that emanates from the physical body. The aura constantly changes, based on our state of mind and mood fluctuations. It is seen or sensed primarily in colors that resonate with the vibratory frequency of the thoughts and emotions of the individual.

Authentic Self—the true or Divine Self (see glossary of Energetic Archetypes) that is the core of our consciousness. The Authentic Self contains and expresses the talents, abilities, and qualities of the soul without the interference of the ego.

Chakra—in Sanskrit, "spinning wheel." These seven vortices of energy located on the etheric energy body are connected with both the front and back of the physical body, supplying it with vital life–force necessary for physical incarnation. The chakras gather and distribute this energy throughout the body. (For more information, see each individual chakra listing.)

Clairaudience—"clear hearing." One of the three inner senses, it is the ability to perceive voices and sounds above the physical threshold. It is a function of the throat chakra.

Clairsentience—"clear feeling." One of the three inner

senses, it is the ability to feel and sense spirit beings and information beyond the physical realm. It is a function of the crown chakra.

Clairvoyance—"clear seeing." One of the three inner senses, clairvoyance is the ability to see into realms beyond the physical. It may or may not involve precognition, which is the ability to know something before it actually occurs. It is a function of the third eye or brow chakra.

Christ Self—the highest vibratory aspect of any soul. The Christ Self is also called the "Higher Self," and is that part of an individual that resonates wholly and completely to the Divine in pure love and unlimited potentiality.

Crown Chakra—chakra seven, corresponding with the top of the head in the physical body. The emotional and spiritual issues associated with it are faith, cosmic awareness, and divine purpose, among others. Its colors are white and violet.

Desire—the combination of will infused with strong emotion. One of the two components necessary for manifestation to occur.

Divine—the Creator God. The core essence of the human soul in all of its perfection.

Ego—the personality. This is in contrast to the Christ Self. In spiritual terms, the ego is the aspect of human consciousness that is primarily fear-based and operates from a perspective of limitation and control.

Etheric Energy Body—the energy body that is closest to the physical one in vibratory density. It is also called the "physical double" because it contains the entire blueprint for the physical body.

Flow—the release of resistance, originating from the ego's need to control. Flow enables us to open fully to our divine purpose and to act in full accordance with the will of the Creator.

Heart Chakra—chakra four, corresponding with the heart,

chest, and arms in the physical body. The emotional and spiritual issues associated with it are love, compassion, forgiveness, generosity and nurturing. Its colors are emerald green and light pink.

Intent—the concentrated focus of will and purpose. One of the two components necessary for manifestation to occur.

Karma—the universal law of cause and effect, which states that a person's thought, words and deeds are always followed by consequences. In the religious teachings of Hinduism and Buddhism, it is believed to be the reason for reincarnation.

Kundalini—latent life-force energy that lies dormant in most individuals until it is awakened by spiritual growth. In Hinduism, the kundalini has been traditionally depicted as a sleeping serpent, coiled around itself three times and residing in the root chakra.

Law of Resonance—simply, like energy attracts like energy. Opposite energies repel one another.

Left brain—the hemisphere of the brain that controls the rational, analytical processes of thinking. Metaphysically, it is considered male (yang).

Reiki—in Japanese, "universal life-force energy." Reiki energy is channeled through the hands of one who has been "attuned" by a Reiki master to the recipient for purposes of healing. There are various hand positions for both the front and back of the body in a full-body Reiki session.

Reincarnation—the process in which the soul takes physical form on the earth plane many times for purposes of meeting and balancing karma.

Right Brain—the hemisphere of the brain that contains sensory receptors for feeling, creativity and mystical experiences. Metaphysically, it is considered female (yin).

Root Chakra—chakra one, which corresponds with the tailbone at the base of the spine in the physical body. The emotional and spiritual issues associated with it are physical presence, tribal identity, safety, security and belonging. Its color is red.

Solar Plexus Chakra—chakra three, which corresponds with the mid-trunk section of the body, between the lower rib cage and the navel. The emotional and spiritual issues associated with it are self-esteem, our perception of personal power and achievement in relation to the outside world. The solar plexus is primary in the absorption of vitality from the sun and the atmosphere. Its color is yellow.

Soul Group—a collection of souls who share similar or identical divine purpose.

Spirit—Divine essence. The life-force that circulates throughout the universe. Synonyms: Creator; Father/Mother God.

Spirit World—the astral or fourth dimension of consciousness. The spirit world is where we go after crossing over at physical death.

Spleen Chakra—chakra two, which corresponds with the area directly below the navel and lower hips. The emotional and spiritual issues associated with it are relationships, emotion, control and sexuality. This chakra also is the seat of the Inner Child, because it resonates with creativity. Its color is orange.

Synchronicity—meaningful coincidence in which two seemingly unrelated events occur at the same time.

Third Eye Chakra—chakra six, which corresponds with the eyes, the area between the eyes and the lower forehead in the physical body. The emotional and spiritual issues associated with it are intuition and psychic ability, perception of both physical and non-physical reality, discernment and reasoning. Its color is indigo.

Throat Chakra—chakra five, which corresponds with the throat, the ears, mouth, jaws and teeth in the physical body. Emotional and spiritual issues associated with it are the expression of one's spirit, including talents, abilities and qualities that the soul has developed through many incarnations. It is also the seat of the will. Its color is light blue.

Visualization—a technique that involves the use of focused imagery in the mind for purposes of manifestation, relaxation and healing.

Will—the exertion of an individual's choices. Will can be either human or divine in nature. One of the goals of spiritual enlightenment is the fusion of the two.

Worlds of Spirit—all of the vibratory planes of consciousness above the physical one.

Glossary of Energetic Archetypes

Achiever—the Self that values accomplishment above all else. Energetically, the Achiever is connected to the solar plexus chakra and is associated with "doing" versus "being."

Divine Self—the soul in all of its perfection.

Father—the archetype of the male parent who expresses qualities of logic, reason, order, strength, structure and labor. This archetype is associated with the left (yang) side of the brain and is universal.

Inner Child—the Self that expresses qualities of innocence, purity, open-mindedness, creativity and sometimes, vulnerability and helplessness. The Inner Child energetically resides in the spleen chakra.

Judge—the Self that is unable to perceive divine reality and potential. The judge is a function of the ego and operates within a limited framework of fear. Its energetic seat is the brow chakra.

Martyr—the Self that demonstrates qualities of self-sacrifice to an extreme, often to its own detriment. Although the martyr appears to be sincere, it operates from an ego basis of fear in its attempts to gain recognition.

Mother—the archetype of the female parent who expresses

qualities of nurturing, compassion, trust, gentleness and unconditional love. This archetype is associated with the right (yin) side of the brain and is universal.

Perfectionist—the Self that is relentlessly driven by the need to control. The Perfectionist operates as an aspect of the ego and results from an imbalance in the solar plexus chakra.

Rescuer—the Self that "validates" itself by helping others temporarily escape responsibility and the consequences of their actions. The Rescuer often shoulders others' karmic lessons and consequently delays their spiritual growth.

Scapegoat—the Self who receives guilt and blame from others. The Scapegoat develops as a consequence of low self-esteem and an imbalance in the solar plexus chakra.

Shadow Selves—the "disowned" or unclaimed qualities of an individual. The Shadow Self is commonly referred to as the "dark" side of the personality and includes fear-based traits such as rage, hatred, jealousy and revenge. When these traits are acknowledged or recognized, they can be integrated and healed by the Divine Self.

Visionary—the Self that is expressed when the brow chakra is unblocked from ego restrictions. The Visionary is able to see, feel and connect with higher vibratory realms of spirit and the Divine Self.

Warrior—the Self that gains power from confrontation and defense in order to protect itself. The Warrior results from an imbalance in either the root chakra, which concerns our tribal identities, or the solar plexus chakra, which is the seat of our personal power.

GB